D0369709

The Hours

David Hare was born in Sussex in 1947. He is one of Britain's most internationally performed playwrights whose work includes *Racing Demon*, *The Absence of War*, *Skylight*, *Amy's View*, *My Zinc Bed* and *Via Dolorosa*. His first work for television *Licking Hitler* won the BAFTA award for the Best Film in 1978 and his first cinema film, *Wetherby*, which he also directed, won the Golden Bear at Berlin in 1985. He has written screenplays for two of his plays, *Plenty* and *The Secret Rapture*, and in 1997 he directed the feature film of Wallace Shawn's *The Designated Mourner*. He is currently adapting Jonathan Franzen's novel *The Corrections*.

The Hours

a screenplay by

David Hare

based on the novel by

Michael Cunningham

faber and faber

First published in the UK in 2003
by Faber and Faber Ltd

3 Queen Square London WC1N 3AU
Published in the United States by Talk Miramax Books, a division of Hyperion, in 2002.

Printed in England by Mackays of Chatham plc, Chatham, Kent

A CIP record for this book
is available from the British Library

ISBN 0–571–21476–2

2 4 6 8 10 9 7 5 3 1

2001
Clarissa Vaughan
Sally Lester
Richard
Barbara
Louis Waters
Julia Vaughan

1951
Laura Brown
Dan Brown
Richie
Kitty
Mrs. Latch
Hotel Clerk

1923 (& 1941)
Virginia Woolf
Leonard Woolf
Nelly Boxall
Lottie Hope
Ralph Partridge
Vanessa Bell
Julian Bell
Angelica Bell
Quentin Bell
Railway Clerk
Maid

Introduction

It was one of Paramount's most prolific producers, Scott Rudin, who asked me to write the screenplay of Michael Cunningham's novel *The Hours*. Scott is the man who has produced, or helped produce, my last five stage plays, and he had bought the film rights to this particular book long before anyone had heard of it, certainly way before it acquired its formidable international reputation. Two years on, I can still recall the immediate feelings of panic and despair induced by Scott first telling me that he had bought an outstanding literary novel, which explored a single day in the lives of three different women at three different periods in the twentieth century. "It is", Scott said, "perfect for you." My heart sank. Here was a film I wasn't going to be able to avoid.

Like most writers who value their freedom, I do everything I can to avoid writing movies. In my leisure time, the cinema remains my most time-consuming passion. Whether haunting the revival houses in Paris, or just dropping by for a regular stopover at my local Odeon in London, I am uncomfortably aware that my wife and I are frequently, by some twenty years, the oldest people in the cinema. I have begun to look round and realize that, unlike nearly all our friends whose adolescence was defined by the forgetful pleasures of the movie-house, we seem to be the only ones who are carrying on regardless. No-one of my age is going to fool themselves into thinking they can recapture the ravishing excitement of an adolescence almost contemporary with the greatest work of Godard, Fellini, Malle and Bergman, but, for me, the cinema remains a delightful combination of off- and on-duty, a place where I still go, from my more usual work in the theatre, both to relax and to learn. Although I wrote and directed three feature films in rapid succession in the 1980s, during one of those rare, exhilarating periods when the British film industry was not cravenly trying to imitate the American—Channel 4, in those days, wanted to show Britain as it was—one of my reasons for stopping was that too much time spent behind the camera was beginning to spoil my appetite for being in the audience. I have, in that wonderful phrase of a French film critic, done "my 20,000 hours in the dark".

When offered the chance to adapt *The Hours*, I was indeed drawn to it immediately, just as Scott had expected, but my reasons were different from his. This was a book which did not belong in any obvious genre. It was startling. Most films, and most Hollywood films in particular, show family likeness pretty early on. Almost from the moment you hear the opening music—a film's most insistent genre-definer—you know instantly what kind of film you are watching. At once you tend to remember how many similar films you have watched before. You could even say it is fundamental to the appeal of film-fiction that, more than any other medium, it is, like the sea, each time different but each time the same. The very familiarity of Western, psycho-thriller, bio-pic and light romance as traditional forms, capable of infinite depth and variation, has enabled artists to climb creatively on one another's shoulders. So many people, after all, have tried to build upwards from Hitchcock, from Hawks, from Griffith and from Eisenstein. But as I started to read Cunningham's three interwoven stories—the author, Virginia Woolf, writing *Mrs. Dalloway* in Richmond, England in 1923 ; the housewife, Laura Brown, despairing of life and of motherhood in Los Angeles in 1951; and the hostess, Clarissa Vaughan, preparing a party for her oldest friend in contemporary New York—I began to feel attracted by the idea of a piece for which, quite simply, there was no model. It was certainly not a conventional women's picture—nobody makes a quilt—nor was it, in any sense, heritage cinema. However well or badly we did it, one thing was sure. A film of *The Hours* was not going overly to resemble anything which had gone before.

There are admittedly a few movies (not very many) with triangular structures, of which *Amores Perros* is one of the most brilliant and the most recent. There are also movies which flash back between historical periods and the present day (*The French Lieutenant's Woman* famously took years to get made because of the intractability of this very problem). And there are movies whose whole point and purpose you cannot understand until the separate strands of their narrative come together. Even so, it is hard to recall another film which finds its inspiration in the writing of a famous book, and which then flashes forward to show the effect that book has had on two people whose lives are separated by almost fifty years. Even on the page, it would be hard to think of a format which, at the outset, appears so unpromising and apparently contrived. But under the grip of Michael Cunningham's firm control, this highly unusual structure not only flows with a surprising inevitability. It also offers deep pleasures of recognition, as you slowly begin to work out for yourself the parallels being drawn between the different worlds.

It is, you may say, a mark of my undiminished respect for the original novel that I had to travel so far in order to restore it. The great mystery of adaptation is that true fidelity can only be achieved through lavish promiscuity. At my first, four-hour meeting with Michael, he made a generous gesture of trust. He observed that, when writing the book, he had simply been trying to organize a large number of themes and stories into patterns which made sense for him. Now, he insisted, the screenwriter should rearrange the material with an equal freedom. Although I was taken aback by his kindness—this was the kind of utopian offer you most want to hear—I had little idea at the time of just how handsomely I intended to take him up on it. I was so drawn to the power of Michael's prose that I remember reading out a passage from the book ("It had seemed like the beginning of happiness, and Clarissa is still sometimes shocked, more than thirty years later, to realize that it *was* happiness . . . Now she knows: That was the moment right then. There has been no other.") and saying I could not conceive of a final film which did not contain those lines. I remember Scott, more experienced at adaptation than I, looking at me shrewdly and saying nothing.

It was certainly our early decision not to resort to voice-over which marked the eventual shape and direction of the script. It is true that nothing is more irritating than when gurus pronounce, with that sententiousness which now marks the professional teaching of screenwriting, that in drama it is always better to show than to tell. These supposed experts in the mysteries of the craft might do well to remember that William Shakespeare, himself the supreme master of showing, made a point of always mixing showing with telling, and of using what we now call stream-of-consciousness in the form of monologue and direct address. The truth is that the best writers use a combination of both. A good film may perfectly well be less memorable for the plight of its characters than for what they have to say about that plight. But anyone approaching the task of adapting Cunningham's novel and finding that so much of the defining action happens inside the characters' heads faces an awkward choice: whether or not to allow any of the three women to speak their thoughts directly to the audience. It was an anxiety that the very *sound* of voice-over would instantly consign the movie into a recognizable genre—the literary film—which made me keen to invent situations which would seek to intimate what Michael had been able to describe directly. It was, of the two available strategies, much the more difficult. But it's one I've never regretted.

The actual drafting and re-drafting of the film took place over the space of a year and was throughout guided and helped in highly enjoyable discussion with Scott Rudin and his co-producer Robert Fox. At the end of that year, we were joined by Stephen Daldry, who had directed me on the sole occasion that I had tried my hand at acting. He came to us straight from the triumph of his first film *Billy Elliot*, and disappeared from time to time to re-decorate his already buckled mantelpiece with yet more gold and silver sculpture from all over the world. It was Stephen's special contribution to make us re-examine the politics of the work and to remind us of an essential element which was making our film more distinctive than perhaps we realized. We were hoping to look full in the face the powerful allure of self-killing. (The tactful gas-tap at the end of William Wyler's great film *Sister Carrie* seemed a long time ago). It was essential we did it in a way which allowed the act its full consequence and reverberation. One of the most powerful parallels in the book is between the devastation of First World War which is still echoing among the bourgeoisie in *Mrs. Dalloway*, and the similar devastation caused by Aids in the gay society of contemporary New York. Stephen was determined that we should achieve a film which not only sought to avoid the stereotyping of its characters' sexuality, but which also found an honest and original way of portraying the disease.

Whether we succeeded remains to be seen. If Hollywood wisdom is right and only second-rate books make great films, then *The Hours* is foredoomed. It was, however, my luck to hand the script on to a cast which was led by Meryl Streep, Julianne Moore and Nicole Kidman and to try to grant them a small fraction at least of the license Michael Cunningham had given me. Everyone knows that for a writer who chooses to stick around for the filming of his work, the experience is roughly the same as that of a doctor who is required to perform a particularly tricky piece of surgery from the gallery upstairs. You can do anything you like except handle the actual instruments. It is measure both of Stephen Daldry and Scott Rudin's patience and seriousness that this, for once, was a set where the writer was welcome. As a result, I was able to respond to the privilege of watching great actors rehearse my material by pushing a scene or a sequence in a far more original direction than the one I had planned in the silence of my study. For a writer the great pleasure of film-making should be the opportunity to do bespoke instead of off-the-peg.

The central, haunting problem of the adaptation was, of course, to keep the three stories equally compelling. Nothing could be more disastrous to the impact of the film than for the audience to end up regretting the time they spent with one set of characters, and wishing they had spent more with another. It was inevitable that with such a difficult balance to be achieved the editing of the film would be long and painstaking, as Stephen worked to make the celluloid leaps between the stories as satisfying as the stories themselves. As I write, I'm only one of three people to have seen the film and I am uniquely disqualified from giving an opinion. But I can say, as I sit watching the weights being once more re-adjusted in the scales, it would be great if film-making was always as interesting as this.

The Hours

1.   EXT. MONK'S HOUSE. RODMELL. ENGLAND.
      DAY.

A river flows, not far from a small house in the Sussex countryside. A card reads 'SUSSEX, ENGLAND. 1941'. It is the 28th March, a desolate, gray morning, as a woman of 59, very thin, in a huge overcoat with a fur collar, comes out of the house and hurries across the lawn. The edge of the lawn turns into grassy, open field as she carries on her way, moving quickly, determinedly towards her destination.

2.   EXT. RIVER OUSE.
      DAY.

The woman reaches an embankment and has to clamber down to a brackish, mud-brown River Ouse. Her elegant, unsuitable shoes stick in the mud. The woman is seen more closely—her face pale, fine, gaunt. As soon as she gets to the river's edge she looks round for a suitable stone. She sees one lying on the ground, the size and shape of a pig's skull. She picks it up and crams it a little clumsily into the pocket of her coat. Then VIRGINIA WOOLF turns and without taking off her shoes begins to wade out into the river.

3.   EXT/INT. MONK'S HOUSE.
      DAY.

LEONARD WOOLF is coming in from the garden on the other side of the house. At this point, he is 61. He has muddy corduroys and a pullover, the very picture of the aging intellectual—austere, ascetic with a fine forehead and glasses. He comes distractedly into a small hallway at the back of the house and starts taking off his wellington boots, unaware of anything wrong.

4.   INT. MONK'S HOUSE. SITTING ROOM.
     DAY.

Two blue envelopes are propped up on the mantelpiece. In handwriting, the single word 'Leonard' is on one; the single word 'Vanessa' on the other. LEONARD'S hand reaches to lift his envelope, leaving the other where it is. He stands, fearful. The sitting room of the house is bohemian, casual, artistic, attractive. A YOUNG MAID comes into the room, unaware of the drama that is about to unfold.

                              MAID
Are you ready for lunch, sir?

                            LEONARD
Not quite. Not just at the moment.

The MAID goes out. LEONARD, still in his gardening clothes, is tense as he opens the envelope. He unfolds two blue pages. VIRGINIA WOOLF'S voice is heard as she reads the letter.

                      VIRGINIA (*voice over*)
Dearest, I feel certain that I am going mad again. I feel we cant go through another of these terrible times. And I shant recover this time. I begin to hear voices and cant concentrate. So I am doing what seems the best thing to do.

LEONARD looks up, alarmed, beginning to panic.

                       VIRGINIA (*v.o.*)
You have given me the greatest possible happiness. You have been in every way all that anyone could be. I know that I am spoiling your life, that without me you could work. And you will, I know.

5.   EXT. MONK'S HOUSE. RODMELL.
     DAY.

LEONARD runs back down to pull on his Wellington boots, then runs out of the back door. He comes out of the house and moves rapidly down the lawn. Terrified, he begins to run as the river comes in sight. Meanwhile :

VIRGINIA (v.o.)

You see, I cant even write this properly. I cant read. What I want to say is that I owe all the happiness of my life to you. You have been entirely patient with me & incredibly good. Everything has gone from me but the certainty of your goodness. I cant go on spoiling your life any longer. I dont think two people could have been happier than we have been.

LEONARD has reached the edge of the river. He sees a woman's foot-prints in the mud. He looks out across its empty, flowing surface.

VIRGINIA (v.o.)

Virginia.

6. EXT. RIVER.
   DAY.

At once the image of **VIRGINIA WOOLF'S** body, face down, swirling fantastically like a catherine wheel, back on the surface of the water and carried along by the current. Her hair is unloosed, her coat has billowed out. Her body swirls, moving fast downstream, wildly festooned like Ophelia, then comes to rest against an underwater pillar and curls up like a baby as the water catches the corpse against the stone. It is caught against the stanchion of a bridge. Over the bridge, in convoy, a line of army trucks is passing, loaded with soldiers in transit. The convoy passes over, ignorant of the corpse beneath the bridge.

7. CREDITS. EXT/INT. THE BROWNS' HOUSE. LOS ANGELES.
   DAWN.

Now a delivery truck moves down a suburban street. A card reads LOS ANGELES. 1951. The credits begin. It is only just past dawn as the truck passes a car coming from the opposite direction. The car approaches a one-level, small detached house, which sits, secure, confident, a familiar image of post-war America. The car draws up in the drive, and from it gets out DAN BROWN, a sturdy, handsome American, just turning 30. He wears suit trousers and a white open-neck shirt, and he is carrying a bunch of white roses. He lets himself in through the front door, and moves, roses in hand, along past the sitting room with its pastel shades and low, sparse furniture into the kitchen. As he reaches for a vase, he looks towards the door of a nearly darkened bedroom which is open at the back of the house. A few rays of light from the window help to pick out shapes. In the bedroom LAURA BROWN, a few years older than DAN, is lying asleep in the bed. She is small, angular and fragile. She turns a moment in her sleep.

8.   CREDITS. EXT. HOGARTH HOUSE. RICHMOND.
      DAWN.

A card reads RICHMOND, ENGLAND 1923. A younger LEONARD WOOLF, only 43, is walking past the church, carrying a newspaper and a pile of envelopes and packages he has collected. This suburban quarter, half an hour away from London, is rich with flowers, lawns, trees. In the other direction come the morning COMMUTERS, dark-coated men, on their way to the station to work. Beside the church is a big gray-stone house, its great face unmoving in the dawn.

9.   CREDITS. INT. HOGARTH HOUSE. HALL & GALLERY.
      DAWN.

LEONARD WOOLF opens the door of the house and goes into the hall, which is lined with paintings. He puts down the packages and paper and looks up in time to see a man in his 60s, obviously a DOCTOR—he carries a doctor's bag and is in a dark coat—coming down the stairs, heading to have a word with him.

LEONARD

Ah, Doctor. Good morning.

DOCTOR

Mr. Woolf. No worse, I think. The main thing is to keep her
where she is, keep her calm.

LEONARD

Mmm. Friday then?

DOCTOR

Friday.

Their conversation is left behind. Upstairs, on the first floor, beyond the
banisters of an open gallery, is the room the DOCTOR has come out of.
Inside the bedroom, a woman is alone. She is lying chastely, blinds down
at the windows. She is the younger VIRGINIA WOOLF, now only 41.
She is staring up at the ceiling.

10. CREDITS. EXT/INT. CLARISSA'S APARTMENT. NEW YORK.
    DAWN.

A card reads NEW YORK CITY, 2001. A subway train rattles violently past,
and a lone WOMAN is left standing on the platform. At street level, the
sun is just about to rise down West 10th, one of the leafiest and most
pleasant streets in the Village. The woman, SALLY LESTER, is walking
quickly down the dawn street, returning home. She is tall, dark, dynamic,
in her late 30s, wearing a leather jacket and jeans. She approaches a high
red-brick terraced house, goes up the steps and lets herself in through its
white-painted front door. SALLY goes up to the first-floor apartment,
which she also unlocks. SALLY walks straight through the living room of
quiet, Bloomsbury-bourgeois homeliness—terracotta and pine, clay pots,
ceramics, plants and massive numbers of books. She goes down a corridor
and into a warm-colored bedroom, light beginning to beat now against
large blinds. SALLY sheds clothes as she goes, taking off her leather jacket
and jeans, stripping down to a T-shirt and knickers. She gets into the bed,

doing nothing to wake the apparently sleeping figure beside her. CLARISSA VAUGHAN is short of 50, tall, splendid beside the smaller SALLY. CLARISSA does not react visibly, but a moment after SALLY closes her eyes, CLARISSA opens hers.

11.   CREDITS. MONTAGE. ALL OF THE ABOVE. ALL DAWN.

2001, 1951 & 1923. In montage, DAN BROWN stands in the bathroom in front of the mirror, tying his tie. CLARISSA throws back the sheet from the bed and gets up. She comes into the small bathroom in her white night gown, ties her hair back behind her head. LAURA, awake now, reaches for a book which is lying at the side of her bed. As her hand reaches for it, the title is clearly seen: *Mrs. Dalloway.* VIRGINIA sits alone in her bedroom in her dressing-gown, looking at herself in the mirror, then lifts her fingers to adjust her hair. Water pours onto CLARISSA'S face in the shower as she reaches her naked arm out in front of her to grope for the tap, invisible in steam. DAN sets out the breakfast things at the kitchen table for three people, then goes and spoons Nescafé for himself into a mug. He pours on hot water. CLARISSA, in a robe, goes to fill her percolator from a kitchen sink which is full of live crabs, in water. VIRGINIA completes dressing, checks herself neatly in the mirror, walks down the corridor and stands for a moment at the top of the stairs, readying herself. CLARISSA comes into her living room, stands in the middle with her remote control and adjusts the lighting, then turns on a classical radio station. LAURA arranges the pillows to enjoy a luxurious few moments of reading. She turns to listen for the sound of her husband in the kitchen.

In succession, the three women, suspended: VIRGINIA pausing, CLARISSA looking around satisfied with the environment she has created, LAURA listening. Then one thing disturbs CLARISSA: a bunch of sorry-looking dead flowers in the corner of the room. She shakes her head in irritation. DAN brings his roses from the sink and puts the vase on the kitchen table. As he does so, another vase is put down by a MAID'S hands, this time with a bunch of blue cornflowers. As it goes down, echoing the identical motion from 28 years later, the credits end.

12. INT. HOGARTH HOUSE. HALL & GALLERY.
DAY.

1923. The vase of cornflowers is seen to be on a table in the open hall of Hogarth House. LEONARD WOOLF is sitting eating toast, drinking coffee, and already reading proof-reading a manuscript. He looks up at the sound of VIRGINIA appearing from upstairs.

VIRGINIA

Good morning, Leonard.

LEONARD

Good morning, Virginia. How was your sleep?

VIRGINIA

Uneventful.

LEONARD

The headaches?

VIRGINIA

No. No headaches.

LEONARD

The doctor seemed pleased.

VIRGINIA helps herself to tea from the table and nods at the mail.

VIRGINIA

That's all from this morning?

LEONARD

Yes. This young man has submitted his manuscript. I've found three errors of fact and two spelling mistakes and I'm not yet on page four.

7

LEONARD is watching her all the time and sees that she is not planning
to sit down.

> LEONARD

Have you had breakfast?

> VIRGINIA

Yes.

> LEONARD

Liar.

LEONARD'S tone is casual. He has the quiet, tactful manner of a good
nurse.

> LEONARD

Virginia, it is not at my insistence. It's the wish of your doctors.

VIRGINIA just looks at him, not answering.

> LEONARD

I'm going to send Nelly up with a bun and some fruit.

Again, VIRGINIA looks at LEONARD, disobediently.

> LEONARD

Very well, then. Lunch. A proper lunch. Husband and wife
sitting down to soup, pudding and all. By force, if necessary.

> VIRGINIA

Leonard, I believe I may have a first sentence.

LEONARD looks her in the eye, knowing how stubborn she is.

> LEONARD

Work, then. But then you must eat.

13. INT. HOGARTH HOUSE. STUDY.
    DAY.

VIRGINIA goes into her plain, serene study and sits down, picking up a board on which she writes. There is an inkwell, a fountain pen. She lights a cigarette. Then, charged with quiet excitement, she opens a clean notebook. The blank page. Then a feeling of pleasure appears on her face in the hushed room. Before writing she tries her sentence out loud.

                    VIRGINIA
    Mrs. Dalloway said she would buy the flowers herself.

14. INT. BROWNS' HOUSE. LOS ANGELES.
    DAY.

1951. LAURA is lying in the bed, luxuriating in a moment of being alone. She reaches for the copy of *Mrs. Dalloway* beside her bed and she opens it. She smiles in anticipated pleasure. She speaks out loud.

                    LAURA
    "Mrs. Dalloway said she would buy the flowers herself."

15. INT. CLARISSA'S APARTMENT. NEW YORK.
    DAY.

2001. CLARISSA is standing in the middle of the living room, frowning, as if wondering what she should do. Then she calls out to SALLY, unseen in the other room.

                    CLARISSA
    Sally! I think I'll buy the flowers myself.

16. INT. CLARISSA'S APARTMENT. BEDROOM.
    DAY.

SALLY still lying in bed blearily reacts to what she has heard.

SALLY

What? What flowers?

And then she remembers what day it is. SALLY starts to get out of bed.

SALLY

Oh shit, I'd forgotten . . .

SALLY falls back on the bed.

17. INT. BROWNS' HOUSE.
    DAY.

1951. A 5-year old boy is watching as cereal is poured into a bowl.
LAURA and DAN'S son, RICHIE, is sitting at the table as DAN pre-
pares his breakfast. RICHIE is in pajamas, a sensitive little boy, his face
unable to censor his shifting feelings. DAN is in shirt and tie, his jacket
neatly hung on the back of a chair.

DAN

There you are son. You're never going to be a big boy if you
don't eat your breakfast.

RICHIE

Is Mommy getting up this morning?

DAN

Of course she is. Of course Mommy's getting up. She just
needs her rest. Look. Here she is.

And indeed, LAURA has now appeared in the doorway, the bulge of an
early to mid-term pregnancy visible. LAURA shakes her head at the sight
of the white roses on the table. There's something odd, distant in her
manner.

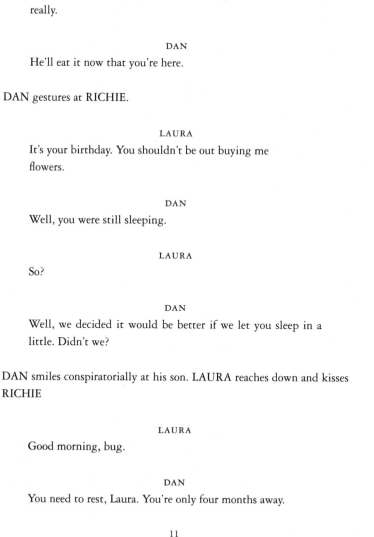

LAURA

Happy birthday.

DAN

Morning, honey.

LAURA

Oh, Dan. Roses. On your own birthday. You're too much, really.

DAN

He'll eat it now that you're here.

DAN gestures at RICHIE.

LAURA

It's your birthday. You shouldn't be out buying me flowers.

DAN

Well, you were still sleeping.

LAURA

So?

DAN

Well, we decided it would be better if we let you sleep in a little. Didn't we?

DAN smiles conspiratorially at his son. LAURA reaches down and kisses RICHIE

LAURA

Good morning, bug.

DAN

You need to rest, Laura. You're only four months away.

11

Honestly! I'm fine. I'm just tired.

DAN touches her stomach tenderly. LAURA smiles, but then slips away. She pours herself coffee. DAN is putting his jacket on over his dazzling white shirt, readying himself for work.

DAN

I've been telling him he's got to eat his breakfast.

LAURA

That's true.

DAN

So it's a beautiful day. What are you two going to be doing with it?

LAURA

Oh, we've got our plans, haven't we?

DAN

What plans?

LAURA

Well, it wouldn't be much of a party, would it, if I told you every detail in advance?

DAN

Then I'd better shut up, hadn't I?

DAN grins at RICHIE, the whole performance for his benefit.

DAN

Hey, is that the time? I'd better get going.

DAN is looking at his watch. It's a morning ritual—the same every day. He gathers his briefcase and heads for the door in haste.

LAURA

Have a good day.

DAN

You too.

LAURA

And Dan . . .

DAN stops at the door.

LAURA

Happy birthday.

DAN

Thank you.

DAN'S gone. Without him, the room feels silent. RICHIE looks at his mother. It's as if she's nervous at being left alone with RICHIE. LAURA waves good-bye to DAN outside in the drive, then turns back to RICHIE.

LAURA

You need to finish your breakfast.

RICHIE

That's what I'm doing.

LAURA comes and sits at the table. RICHIE watches her, expectant.

LAURA

So. I'm going to make a cake. That's what I'm going to do. I'm going to make the cake for Daddy's birthday.

RICHIE

Mommy, can I help?

LAURA

Well . . .

RICHIE

Can I help make the cake?

LAURA frowns a second, as if regretting her son's eagerness.

LAURA

Of course you can, sweet pea. I'm not going to do anything
without you.

18. INT. CLARISSA'S APARTMENT.
     DAY.

SALLY appears from the bedroom and looks down to the living room
where she sees CLARISSA can be heard on the phone. SALLY is pulling
on her jeans. The whole apartment is submerged in books—bound proofs,
hardbacks and manuscripts.

CLARISSA

No, of course you must come. I mean it. I always wanted you
to come. And everyone involved in the actual ceremony.

CLARISSA acknowledges SALLY with a wave of the hand. SALLY turns
and goes into the kitchen while CLARISSA goes back to the phone.

CLARISSA

I don't know. Around sixty. Well it will, it will mean so much.
The whole occasion. And so the least I can do is have you all to
dinner. Just to say thank you. I mean it. Of course.

SALLY is gone into the kitchen to pour hot coffee. She looks into the sink
at the wriggling crabs.

SALLY

My God, what if nobody comes? I suppose we can live for a
month off crustaceans.

SALLY comes back into the room with her coffee and watches
CLARISSA, who is still working her charm on the phone. SALLY mimics
her, wordlessly.

CLARISSA

Oh, I take that as a yes. Oh, that's great. I'm thrilled. Oh,
good.

SALLY smiles affectionately at how characteristic of CLARISSA this
whole conversation has been.

19. EXT. WEST 10TH STREET. NEW YORK.
    DAY.

2001. The sun is shining as CLARISSA appears at the top of the little run
of steps from her apartment and heads cheerfully out onto 10th Street. It's
a dazzling day.

20. EXT. WASHINGTON SQUARE.
    DAY.

CLARISSA heads down Fifth Avenue in good spirits. Rappers go by,
skate-boarders. A few PASSERS-BY greet her as she moves through the
district, a familiar figure, at ease in her favorite quarter. She is on a mobile
phone, still making her arrangements for the party.

CLARISSA

This is Clarissa Vaughan. Yes, I'm just confirming that you're
sending the car to pick me up first. Yeah, and then we're
going . . .

NEIGHBOR

Hi, Clarissa!

CLARISSA

Hi, Hi, can't talk.

CLARISSA waves and returns to her mobile.

CLARISSA

And then we're going over to six seventy-five Hudson. That's right. Between fourteenth and ninth. Then uptown. And there I will need you to wait. And it'll be over at seven.

21. EXT. SPRING STREET.
    DAY

Now CLARISSA is pausing for traffic and walking across Spring Street towards an exquisite flower shop, which is decked in buckets of summer blooms. CLARISSA heads cheerfully towards the glass door and goes in.

22. INT. FLOWER SHOP.
    DAY

CLARISSA goes into the chic little flower shop and raises her arms a little to greet the owner. Her name is BARBARA—in her fifties, pale, with dark hair.

CLARISSA

Flowers! What a beautiful morning!

BARBARA kisses CLARISSA and puts an arm round her, the two of them at ease.

BARBARA

Clarissa, hi! How are you?

CLARISSA

I'm having a party! My friend Richard's won the Carrouthers.

BARBARA

Well, that's just terrific. If I knew what it was.

CLARISSA

It's a poetry prize. For a life's work. It's the most prestigious. For a poet it's the best you can do.

BARBARA

Oh. Very good.

CLARISSA is proud on Richard's behalf but BARBARA is already pointing along the rows of flowers.

BARBARA

So what would you like? We've got loads of lilies . . .

CLARISSA

No. Too morbid. Hydrangeas, I think. And let's just have buckets of roses. Whatever. To hell with it. Spare no expense.

CLARISSA picks out one bunch of flowers.

CLARISSA

I'm going to take these with me.

BARBARA gets out armfuls of yellow roses and takes them to the desk, while an ASSISTANT takes the ones CLARISSA has picked out to take back herself. CLARISSA wanders up the other end. Now BARBARA is cutting the stalks and wrapping them.

BARBARA

I actually tried to read Richard's novel.

CLARISSA

Oh, did you? I know it's not easy.

BARBARA smiles, not unkindly, at the understatement.

CLARISSA

I know. It did take him ten years to write.

BARBARA

Yeah, well, I figured. Maybe it just takes another ten to read.

CLARISSA just smiles, coming to the counter to collect her flowers.

BARBARA

It's you, isn't it?

CLARISSA

What is?

BARBARA

In the novel? Isn't it meant to be you?

CLARISSA

Oh I see. Yeah.

CLARISSA shrugs, half pleased, half embarrassed.

CLARISSA

I mean, in a way. Sort of. Richard's a writer. That's what he is. He uses things which actually happen.

BARBARA

Yes.

CLARISSA

And years ago, he and I were students, it's true. But then he changes things.

BARBARA

Sure.

CLARISSA

I don't mean in a bad way.

BARBARA looks at her a moment. CLARISSA frowns.

CLARISSA

More like, he makes them his own.

23. INT. HOGARTH HOUSE. STUDY.
    DAY.

1923. VIRGINIA WOOLF sits in her study, pen poised. She speaks to herself.

VIRGINIA

A woman's whole life . . .

24. EXT. SPRING STREET.
    DAY.

CLARISSA comes out of the flower shop, carrying a bunch of flowers and sets off down the street. VIRGINIA continues speaking underneath.

VIRGINIA (*v.o.*)

. . . in a single day . . .

25. INT. BROWNS' HOUSE. KITCHEN.
    DAY.

1951. LAURA sits thinking at the kitchen-table, turning the pages of a cookery book.

                    VIRGINIA (*v.o.*)
    Just one day . . . and in that day, her whole life.

RICHIE has run across the kitchen and now climbs onto his mother's lap.

26. EXT. TRIANGLE BUILDING.
    DAY.

2001. Now CLARISSA is walking through the meat-market, carrying her distinctive bunch of flowers. She crosses the road among the meat trucks. And then she approaches the huge red-painted triangular building which looms up at her from the crossroads.

27. INT. RICHARD'S APARTMENT.
    DAY.

At an upstairs window a MAN in a dressing gown parts his curtain to look down at CLARISSA approaching.

28. INT/EXT. TRIANGLE BUILDING.
    DAY.

CLARISSA, confident, cheerful, approaches a doorway crammed between the metal criss-crossings of fire-escapes. She opens the door with a key and goes into a tiny, squalid, airless lobby. A fluorescent panel splutters on the ceiling. CLARISSA heads for the cheerless graffiti-strewn freight elevator, closes the gate and rides upwards.

29. INT. RICHARD'S APARTMENT & CORRIDOR.
DAY.

CLARISSA rings the bell of RICHARD'S apartment, then presses her face close to the door to listen.

RICHARD (*inside*)

Mrs. Dalloway, it's you.

CLARISSA

Yes, it's me.

RICHARD (*inside*)

Come in.

CLARISSA turns the lock with her own key and goes in to a desolate loft-space. The first space is in near-darkness, a gloomy kitchen-bathroom area. CLARISSA picks her way carefully through to the second, larger space— the living area—where the man at the window is sitting, pale, stick-limbed, in a rotting armchair which is covered in towels. RICHARD is in his late 40s, gaunt from Aids, a noble skull merely, his boxer's nose and high forehead lit by a streak of light from between the blinds. He is wearing a blue robe with child-like drawings of rockets and astronauts on it. The whole place is bleached, chaotic, more or less bare of ornament. This is a man who has pared his life down to very little.

CLARISSA puts down the flowers and goes to the blinds.

CLARISSA

Richard, it's a beautiful morning. How about I let in a little light?

RICHARD

Is it still morning?

CLARISSA

It is.

CLARISSA raises one of the shades. RICHARD barely moves to greet the light.

RICHARD

Have I died? Am I alive?

CLARISSA bends over and kisses his forehead.

RICHARD

Good morning, my dear.

CLARISSA

Any visitors?

RICHARD

Yes.

CLARISSA

Are they still here?

RICHARD

No. They've gone.

CLARISSA

How did they look?

RICHARD

Today? Sort of like black fire. I mean, sort of light and dark at the same time. There was one a bit like an electrified jelly-fish.

CLARISSA looks at him a moment, then picks up the flowers.

RICHARD

They were singing. It may have been Greek.

CLARISSA

You don't sleep at all, do you?

RICHARD

Oh, sleep.

CLARISSA has gone into the kitchen and calls back through to him.

CLARISSA

I saw three bluebirds on the way over. Do you think it's a good
omen?

RICHARD

Do you believe in omens? Omens would mean someone was
looking after us, someone was watching. Do you believe anyone's watching? Do they send *signs*?

RICHARD makes a sort of grin, amused at the idea.

RICHARD

I mean, I'd love to believe it.

CLARISSA

The ceremony's at five. Do you remember?

RICHARD

Do I? Do I remember?

CLARISSA

Then the party's after.

CLARISSA has arranged the flowers and now she re-appears in the doorway of Richard's room. CLARISSA looks at him tolerantly, the long-suf-
fering look of nurse to patient. His complex cocktail of pills is laid out
neatly on a table nearby.

CLARISSA

They did bring you breakfast, didn't they?

RICHARD

What a question. Of course.

CLARISSA

You did eat it, Richard?

RICHARD

Well can you see it? Is there any breakfast lying around?

CLARISSA

I can't see it.

RICHARD

Well, then, I must have eaten it, mustn't I?

CLARISSA

I suppose.

RICHARD

Does it matter?

CLARISSA

Of course it matters. You know what the doctors say. Have you been skipping pills?

CLARISSA is frowning mistrustfully at the way the cocktail is laid out on the table but RICHARD is suddenly impatient, ignoring the question.

RICHARD

Clarissa, I can't take this.

CLARISSA

Take what?

RICHARD

Having to be proud and brave in front of everybody.

CLARISSA

Honey, it's not a performance.

RICHARD

Of course it is. I got the prize for my performance.

CLARISSA

Well, that is nonsense.

RICHARD

I got the prize for having AIDS and going nuts and being brave about it. I actually got the prize for having come through.

CLARISSA

It's not true.

RICHARD

For surviving. *That's* what I got the prize for. You think they'd give it to me if I were healthy?

CLARISSA

Well, yes, as a matter of fact I do.

RICHARD looks at her with an ironic gleam of doubt.

RICHARD

Is it here somewhere?

CLARISSA

What?

RICHARD

The prize. I'd like to look at it.

CLARISSA

You haven't gotten it yet. It's tonight.

RICHARD

Are you sure? I remember the ceremony perfectly. I seem to have fallen out of time.

CLARISSA waits a moment, trying to be patient.

CLARISSA

Richard, it's a party. It's only a party. Populated entirely by people who respect and admire you.

RICHARD

Ah, small party, is it? Select party, is it?

CLARISSA

Your friends.

RICHARD

I thought I lost all my friends. I thought I drove my friends crazy.

RICHARD reaches out and touches the flowers.

RICHARD

"Oh Mrs. Dalloway, always giving parties to cover the silence . . ."

CLARISSA is stunned a moment by his unkindness, and then rallies, keeping her anger at bay.

CLARISSA

Richard, you won't need to *do* anything. All you have to do is appear, sit on the sofa. And I will be there. This is a group of people who want to tell you your work's going to live.

RICHARD

Is it? Is my work going to live?

RICHARD looks at her without pity.

RICHARD

I can't go through with it, Clarissa.

CLARISSA

Why do you say that?

RICHARD

I can't.

CLARISSA

Why?

RICHARD

Because I wanted to be a writer, that's all.

CLARISSA

So?

RICHARD gets up, heaving himself across the room on a crutch.

RICHARD

I wanted to write about it all. Everything that's happening in a moment. The way those flowers looked when you carried them in your arms—this towel, how it smells, how it feels— this thread—all our feelings, yours and mine. The history of who we once were. Everything that's in the world. Everything mixed up. Like it's all mixed up now.

RICHARD'S eyes fill with tears.

RICHARD

And I failed. I failed. Whatever you start with, it ends up so
much less. Sheer fucking pride and stupidity.

RICHARD slumps down again. CLARISSA watches, part impatient, part
helpless.

RICHARD

We want everything, don't we?

CLARISSA

Yes. I suppose we do.

RICHARD

You kissed me on a beach . . .

CLARISSA

Yes.

RICHARD

You remember?

CLARISSA

Of course.

RICHARD

How many years ago?

CLARISSA shakes her head, too overwhelmed to answer.

RICHARD

What did you want then?

Again, CLARISSA says nothing. She is as upset as he is.

RICHARD

Come here, come closer, would you please?

I'm right here.

RICHARD

Take my hand.

CLARISSA takes his painfully thin hand, a handful of twigs.

RICHARD

Would you be angry?

CLARISSA

Would I be angry if you didn't show up at the party?

RICHARD

No. Would you be angry if I died?

CLARISSA

If you died? Would I be angry if you *died*?

RICHARD

Who's this party for?

CLARISSA

What do you mean? Who's it *for*? What are you asking? What are you trying to say?

RICHARD

I'm not trying to say anything! I'm saying!

CLARISSA is panicking now.

RICHARD

I think I'm only staying alive to satisfy you.

CLARISSA is looking at him, aghast.

CLARISSA

So? Well? That's what we do. That's what people do. They stay alive for each other. The doctors told you: you don't need to die. The doctors told you that. You can live like this for years.

RICHARD

Well exactly.

RICHARD smiles, bitterly. CLARISSA shakes her head, firm now.

CLARISSA

I don't accept this. I don't accept what you're saying.

RICHARD

Oh, what? and it's you to decide is it?

CLARISSA

No.

RICHARD

How long have you been doing this?

CLARISSA

Doing what?

RICHARD

How many years, coming to the apartment? What about your own life? What about Sally? Just wait till I die. Then you'll have to think of yourself.

CLARISSA doesn't answer. RICHARD smiles, sure of his point.

RICHARD

How are you going to like that?

CLARISSA lets go of his hand, disturbed. RICHARD just looks at her. CLARISSA gets up and stands a moment, shaken. Then speaks quietly.

CLARISSA

Richard, it would be great if you did come. If you felt well enough to come. Just to let you know: I'm making the crab thing. Not that I imagine it makes any difference.

RICHARD

Of course it makes a difference. I love the crab thing.

CLARISSA is about to leave but RICHARD calls across to her.

RICHARD

Clarissa?

CLARISSA

Yes?

RICHARD raises his head slightly for her to kiss him. CLARISSA puts her lips next to his, with great tenderness, not to hurt him. Then she squeezes his shoulder.

CLARISSA

I'll come back at three-thirty to help you get dressed.

RICHARD

Wonderful.

CLARISSA goes out. The sound of the apartment door being re-opened and then closed. RICHARD is alone.

RICHARD

Wonderful.

30. INT. APARTMENT BLOCK. ELEVATOR.
    DAY.

CLARISSA, in her dark glasses, gets back into the freight elevator, distraught from her encounter. She throws her head back in despair at the side of the elevator. The elevator goes down.

31. INT. HOGARTH HOUSE. VIRGINIA'S STUDY.
    DAY.

1923. VIRGINIA WOOLF is still at her desk, just as before. But now the first pages of her notebook are filled with handwriting. She speaks again to herself.

                    VIRGINIA
    It's on this day, this day of all days, her fate becomes clear to
    her . . .

At once there is a loud knock at the door, interrupting VIRGINIA'S thoughts. Without waiting for an answer, NELLY BOXALL appears. She is large, red-faced, regal, in cook's apron.

                    NELLY
    Excuse me, Mrs. Woolf, Mr. Woolf said I was to come and
    speak to you.

                    VIRGINIA
    I can't imagine why he said that.

NELLY, unyielding, ignores VIRGINIA'S tone.

                    VIRGINIA
    I'm nearly finished, Nelly. Please attend me in the kitchen and
    I'll be down very soon.

32. INT. HOGARTH HOUSE. CORRIDOR & KITCHEN.
     DAY.

VIRGINIA is coming downstairs. She stops, standing with her back
against the wall in the corridor outside the kitchen, preparing herself for
the encounter ahead. From inside she can hear NELLY chattering freely
with LOTTIE.

NELLY

What happens is, she says she wants something then it turns
out she doesn't . . .

LOTTIE

Well she never does, does she? Never wants anything.

NELLY

Especially when she's asked for it. That's a sure sign.

LOTTIE

I wish I'd been there.

NELLY

Yeah, I wish you had, too.

The two women laugh cheerfully. VIRGINIA summons up her courage.

LOTTIE

Did you give her that look? That sort of look you do?

NELLY

I said "Madam . . .

But before NELLY can finish, VIRGINIA has stepped into the open door
and cut her off. NELLY is rolling out pastry and cutting huge chunks of
raw lamb. Beside her, LOTTIE is working. She is in her teens, dressed
identically to NELLY, and collusive, not missing a trick.

33

                    VIRGINIA

Yes, Nelly, tell me, how can I help?

VIRGINIA moves towards the table, trying to take charge of her formidable servant.

                     NELLY

It's about lunch.

                    VIRGINIA

Ah, yes.

                     NELLY

I just had to go ahead on my own.

                    VIRGINIA

I understand.

VIRGINIA recoils slightly at the sight and smell of raw meat.

                    VIRGINIA

You chose a pie?

                     NELLY

I chose a lamb pie.

                    VIRGINIA

That seems suitable.

                     NELLY

You being so busy with your writing.

VIRGINIA does not respond. LOTTIE works on, impassive.

                     NELLY

I had no instructions. And I thought some of them yellow
pears for pudding, unless you'd like something fancier.

VIRGINIA

Pears will be fine.

NELLY lifts up pastry and folds it into the pan, a figure of righteous hard work.

VIRGINIA

You do remember that my sister is coming at four with the family?

NELLY

Yes ma'am, I haven't forgotten.

VIRGINIA

China tea, I think. And ginger.

NELLY hesitates in her actions. LOTTIE registers the moment also.

NELLY

Ginger, madam?

VIRGINIA

I'd like to give the children a treat.

NELLY

We'd have to go to London for ginger ma'am. I haven't finished this and there's the rest of the lunch to get ready.

VIRGINIA steels herself, not rising to the bait.

VIRGINIA

The twelve-thirty train, Nelly, will get you to London just after one. If you return on the two-thirty, you will be back in Richmond soon after three. Do I miscalculate?

NELLY

No.

Well then.

It's a trial of strength. NELLY doesn't move.

Well then? Is something detaining you, Nelly?

VIRGINIA is tense. But she knows she's won. NELLY puts down the rolling pin.

I can't think of anything more exhilarating than a trip to London.

33. INT. HOGARTH HOUSE. PRINTING ROOM. DAY.

VIRGINIA descends the stairs to the print room. The room is overflowing with manuscripts. In the middle of the untidiness, LEONARD sits with a scowl, scrutinizing proofs. Beside him, a handsome young man, RALPH PARTRIDGE, is working at the inky hand-operated printing press.

Good morning.

Good morning, Mrs. Woolf.

RALPH looks up, relieved to see her. The atmosphere is extremely tense.

We shall publish no more new authors. I have to tell you I have discovered ten errors in the first proof.

VIRGINIA

Lucky to have found them, then, Leonard.

LEONARD

"Paschendale was a charnel-house from which no min returned." Do you think it is possible that bad writing actually attracts a higher incidence of error?

VIRGINIA is smiling.

VIRGINIA

If it's all right, I thought I might take a short walk.

LEONARD

Not far?

VIRGINIA

No. Just for air.

LEONARD now gives imperceptible consent—just with his eyes.

LEONARD

Go then. If I could walk mid-morning, I'd be a very happy man.

VIRGINIA pauses a moment at the barb, then goes. RALPH watches.

34. EXT. PARADISE ROAD.
    DAY.

There is a school next to Hogarth House and children in the playground. VIRGINIA comes along the pavement in front of the railings, lost in a world of her own. She walks a little, then stops, without realizing, and talks to herself.

VIRGINIA

She'll die. She's going to die. That's what's going to happen.

A couple of people pass, noticing that this vague, genteel woman is talking to herself. Now VIRGINIA stares at a couple of little SCHOOL-GIRLS in the playground, one earnestly whispering to the other, both intent.

VIRGINIA

That's it. She will kill herself. She will kill herself over something which doesn't seem to matter.

35. INT. KITCHEN. BROWNS' HOUSE.
DAY.

1951. LAURA is still in her dressing gown, but now with an apron tied over it. She is sitting frowning at a recipe book on the surface in front of her. Beside her she has assembled all the elements of cake-making—eggs, tins, sugar and a series of pale blue bowls. But the endeavor is stalled. RICHIE is standing beside her, waiting patiently.

LAURA

Let's think.

RICHIE

You grease the pan, Mommy.

LAURA

I know you grease the pan, sweet one. Even Mommy knows that.

Decisively she reaches to assemble the elements. RICHIE frowns, watching.

LAURA

OK. This is what we're going to do. Flour. Bowl. Sifter.

RICHIE

Can I do it, Mommy?

LAURA

Can you sift the flour?

LAURA smiles at him.

LAURA

Yes, you can sift the flour, baby, if that's what makes you happy.

RICHIE

I'd like to.

LAURA

OK. You do that.

LAURA gives RICHIE a sieve, then pours the raw flour in for him to shake out. RICHIE concentrates with great seriousness. Flour falls through the sieve in a fine white powder into a blue china bowl.

LAURA

Isn't it beautiful? Don't you think it looks like snow?

LAURA has gone back to looking at the recipe book again.

LAURA

Next—now this is the next thing. I'm going to show you. The next thing is we measure out the cups.

RICHIE

Mommy, it isn't that difficult.

LAURA

I know, sweet pea. I know it isn't difficult. It's just . . . I want to do this for Daddy.

Because it's his birthday.

That's right. We're baking the cake to show him we love him.

Otherwise he won't know we love him?

LAURA looks at her son a moment.

That's right.

36. INT. CLARISSA'S APARTMENT.
     DAY.

CLARISSA is sitting immobilized in the second bedroom. The room is
stacked with spare furniture which has been cleared away to make room
for the party. CLARISSA has sat down on a hard chair, still trying to
recover from her earlier encounter with RICHARD. Through the front
door, full of cheerfulness, comes SALLY, carrying armfuls of dry cleaning
and a load of Balducci bags.

SALLY

I got all the stuff. My God, what a zoo. Why do people have to
talk about dry cleaning? I mean what is there to talk about?

SALLY has gone straight through to their own bedroom to put the dry
cleaning down on the bed. Now SALLY has come out into the corridor
and is heading with the shopping bags towards the kitchen.

SALLY

I bought you some flowers.

SALLY sees she has been pre-empted by the abundant flowers CLARISSA

40

has already brought home. She throws her own offering down beside them.

SALLY

Where are you?

CLARISSA

In here.

SALLY has put the bags down in the kitchen, and is beginning to get oranges out of them.

SALLY

I got somebody to cover for me at work. I'll be with you all night.

SALLY opens the fridge door and starts putting oranges inside. She frowns slightly at the silence from CLARISSA.

SALLY

Are you all right?

CLARISSA

Sure.

SALLY smiles to herself, not worried by CLARISSA'S slump.

SALLY

I guess you saw Richard.

CLARISSA

That's right.

SALLY

Well, of course. I bet he said "Oh by the way, honey, d'you mind, can I skip the party?"

CLARISSA nods resignedly at SALLY'S prescience. In the other room, SALLY, still unloading oranges, nods in psychic response.

SALLY

Don't worry. Finally. He always shows up.

CLARISSA

Oh sure.

SALLY

In the end. What, Richard miss an award? A chance to talk about his work? I don't think so. He'll show up.

SALLY, in perpetual motion, has now come upon the table-party plan, a mixture of names and circles, which is laid out on the kitchen table.

SALLY

You did the seating.

CLARISSA

I did.

SALLY

I don't believe it. Louis Waters. Richard's Louis? Is he coming?

CLARISSA

He is.

SALLY

You put me next to him. Why do I always get to sit next to the ex's? Is this a hint, sweetheart? Anyway, shouldn't ex's have a table of their own? Where they can all ex together. In exquisite agony.

SALLY has appeared at the jamb of the second bedroom. CLARISSA looks up.

SALLY

I'm off. Try not to pass out from excitement. Clarissa, it's going to be beautiful.

CLARISSA

Thank you.

SALLY

No problem.

SALLY turns and goes out. CLARISSA is alone. The apartment is silent.

CLARISSA

Why is everything wrong?

37. INT. BROWNS' HOUSE.
DAY.

1951. LAURA is looking at the finished cake. It isn't what she'd hoped. She has tried to pipe out the message *HAPPY BIRTHDAY DAN* on top. But the lettering is clumsy, and there are crumbs in the icing. LAURA speaks under her breath.

LAURA

It didn't work. Damn! It didn't work.

At once there is the sound of the back doorbell. LAURA looks, seeing the outline of a woman at the door. She begins to panic, checking in the mirror, alarmed to see herself, still in her bathrobe, looking like a distressed person. RICHIE has come running in, holding a red plastic toy he has been playing with.

RICHIE

Mommy! Mommy! There's someone at the door.

38. INT/EXT. BROWNS' HOUSE.
     DAY.

Just a few seconds later. LAURA swings open the door, having made a
hurried attempt at normality. Her hair is tidier, but she is still in the
robe. At the back door

KITTY is standing, a little younger than LAURA, and more confident,
with a voluptuous, good-looking presence: well made-up, well turned out,
at ease.

LAURA

Hi, Kitty!

KITTY

Hi. Am I interrupting?

LAURA

Of course not. Come in.

KITTY

Are you all right?

KITTY comes through the door. It's true: LAURA looks a little wild-
eyed, desperate.

LAURA

Why, sure.

KITTY

Hi, Richie!

LAURA

Sit down. I've got coffee on. Would you like some?

KITTY

Please.

44

RICHIE is on the floor, observing from a distance. KITTY sits at the kitchen table and sees the sugary heap.

KITTY

Oh look—you made a cake.

LAURA

I know. It didn't work. I thought it was going to work. I thought it would work better than that.

KITTY

Honestly, Laura, I don't know why you find it so difficult.

LAURA

I don't know either.

KITTY

Anyone can make a cake.

LAURA

I know.

KITTY

Everyone can. It's ridiculously easy. Like I bet you didn't grease the pan.

LAURA

I greased the pan.

KITTY smiles. LAURA is getting cups, pouring coffee.

KITTY

All right, but you have other virtues. And Dan loves you so much he won't even notice. Whatever you do, he's going to say it's wonderful.

LAURA looks at her reproachfully and pushes KITTY'S coffee across to her.

Well it's true.

LAURA

Does Ray have a birthday?

KITTY

Sure he does.

LAURA

When is it?

KITTY

September. We go to the country club. We *always* go to the country club. We drink Martinis and spend the day with fifty people.

LAURA

Ray's got a lot of friends.

KITTY

He does.

LAURA

You've both have a lot of friends. You're good at it.

LAURA has said this without envy, and KITTY smiles, accepting the compliment.

LAURA

How is Ray? I haven't seen him in a while.

KITTY

Ray's fine. Hmm.

They both smile.

These guys are something, aren't they?

You can say that again. They came home from the war, they deserved it, didn't they? After what they'd been through?

What did they deserve?

I don't know. Us, I guess. All this.

LAURA gestures round the prosperous surroundings. KITTY nods at the copy of *Mrs. Dalloway* on the kitchen top.

Oh. You're reading a book?

Yeah.

What's this one about?

Oh, it's about this woman who's incredibly . . . well, she's a hostess and she's incredibly confident. And she's going to give a party. And . . . maybe, because she's confident, everyone thinks she's fine. But she isn't.

KITTY has picked up the book and now takes a glance at LAURA. The talk's run out.

So.

KITTY

Well.

LAURA

What is it? Is something wrong, Kitty?

KITTY gathers herself for a moment.

KITTY

I have to go into the hospital for a couple of days.

LAURA

Kitty . . .

KITTY

I have some kind of growth in . . . in my uterus. They're going
to go in and take a look.

LAURA

When?

KITTY

This afternoon.

LAURA just looks at her, not knowing how to respond.

KITTY

I need you to feed the dog.

LAURA

Of course.

There's a moment's silence. KITTY puts her front door key on the kitchen
table.

LAURA

Is that what you came to ask?

KITTY just looks at her, not answering.

LAURA

What did the doctor say, exactly?

KITTY

It's probably what the trouble's been. About getting pregnant.

KITTY looks at LAURA a moment, unused to confidences.

KITTY

The thing is, I mean, you know, I've been really happy with Ray, but well . . . now it turns out there was a reason . . . there was a reason I couldn't conceive. You're lucky, Laura. I don't think you can call yourself a woman until you're a mother.

LAURA looks down at her own stomach. KITTY looks away.

KITTY

The joke is: all my life I could do everything—I mean, I can do anything—really—I never had any trouble—except the one thing I wanted.

LAURA

Yes.

KITTY

That's all.

LAURA

Well at least now they'll be able to deal with it.

KITTY

That's right. That's what they're doing.

LAURA

That's right.

KITTY is rubbing her thumb against her forefinger, as at an imaginary stain.

> KITTY
>
> I'm not worried. What would be the point of worrying?

> LAURA
>
> No. It's not in your hands.

> KITTY
>
> That's it. It's in the hands of some physician I've never met . . .

> LAURA
>
> Kitty . . .

> KITTY
>
> . . . some *surgeon* who probably drinks even more Martinis than Ray, and no doubt always takes a six-iron to the green. Whatever *that* may mean.

KITTY is losing it now, fighting to control her feelings.

> KITTY
>
> I mean, of course I'm worried for Ray.

> LAURA
>
> Come here.

But in fact it is LAURA who gets up and goes over to KITTY. She bends down and embraces her. After a moment, KITTY slips her arms round Laura's waist. The two women hold on to each other, LAURA almost kneeling to be at Kitty's level. Then, without planning it, LAURA kisses Kitty's forehead, lingeringly. KITTY lets her.

> KITTY
>
> I'm doing fine. Really.

LAURA

I know you are.

KITTY

If anything, I'm more worried about Ray. He's not good at this
stuff.

LAURA

Forget about Ray for a minute. Just forget about Ray.

KITTY'S face is against Laura's breasts. She seems to relax into her.
LAURA lifts KITTY'S face, and puts her lips against hers. They both
know what they are doing. They kiss, letting themselves go a moment.
Then KITTY pulls away.

KITTY

You're sweet.

There is a brief moment, then LAURA turns and her eye falls on RICHIE
who is on the floor with his toys. They had both forgotten him. He has
watched throughout. KITTY stands up.

KITTY

You know the routine, right? Half a can in the evening, and
check the water now and then. Ray will feed him in the
morning.

KITTY has got up to go.

LAURA

Kitty, you didn't mind?

KITTY

What? I didn't mind what?

LAURA stands, anxious.

LAURA

Do you want me to drive you?

KITTY

I think I'll feel better if I drive myself.

LAURA

Kitty, it's going to be all right.

KITTY

Of course it is. 'Bye.

KITTY goes out. LAURA stands in the middle of the kitchen. She looks
down at RICHIE who is still looking silently up at her.

LAURA

What? What do you want?

It is said just sharply enough to make RICHIE turn and go silently to his
own room. LAURA looks at him going, then walks across to the kitchen
top. Then, needing to do something decisive, LAURA picks up the cake
which is cooling on a rack. LAURA opens a pedal bin with her foot, and
slides the cake off the plate cleanly into the bin. It makes a satisfyingly
solid noise as it lands.

39. INT. HOGARTH HOUSE. PRINTING ROOM.
    DAY.

1923. In the printing room, RALPH and LEONARD are reading proofs
silently. LOTTIE appears at the door.

LOTTIE

Mr. Woolf, Mrs. Bell has arrived.

LEONARD

Mrs. Bell?

LEONARD looks up in exasperation, as if this were typical.

LEONARD

Not due till 4.

LOTTIE

I can't help that. She's here.

40. INT. HOGARTH HOUSE. DRAWING ROOM. DAY.

Virginia's sister, VANESSA BELL, is waiting in the drawing room. Although, at 44, VANESSA is older than Virginia, she looks younger and more open, more glossy and easygoing. She is just sending her little daughter out to play in the garden as VIRGINIA arrives, followed by LOTTIE.

VANESSA

Virginia!

They kiss. VIRGINIA laughs conspiratorially.

VIRGINIA

Leonard thinks it's the end of civilization. People you invite at four who come at two thirty . . .

VANESSA

Oh, God.

VIRGINIA

Barbarians!

VANESSA

We finished lunch earlier than we imagined.

VIRGINIA

I've had to pack Nelly off to London for sugared ginger.

VIRGINIA is heading cheerfully out towards the garden, but VANESSA comments well within LOTTIE'S hearing.

> VANESSA
>
> Oh Virginia, you're not still frightened of the servants!

LOTTIE is left smiling, as the two women head into the garden.

41. EXT. HOGARTH HOUSE. GARDEN.
     DAY

VIRGINIA and VANESSA are sitting in the garden at Hogarth House, watching the children playing.

> VIRGINIA
>
> And how are you, sister?

> VANESSA
>
> Frantic. It's been ridiculous in London.

> VIRGINIA
>
> Ridiculous how?

> VANESSA
>
> Busy.

> VIRGINIA
>
> Why is busy ridiculous?

> VANESSA
>
> I would have invited you to our party, but I knew you wouldn't come.

> VIRGINIA
>
> Did you?

VIRGINIA looks genuinely surprised.

> VIRGINIA
>
> How did you know that?

> VANESSA
>
> I thought you never came to town.

> VIRGINIA
>
> You no longer ask me.

> VANESSA
>
> Aren't you forbidden to come? Do the doctors not forbid it?

> VIRGINIA
>
> The doctors!

> VANESSA
>
> Do you not pay heed to your doctors?

> VIRGINIA
>
> Not when they are a bunch of contemptible Victorians.

VANESSA looks sideways at VIRGINIA, surprised by her forthrightness.

> VANESSA
>
> So? What are you saying? Are you feeling better? Has this fastness made you stronger?

> VIRGINIA
>
> I'm saying, Vanessa, that even crazy people like to be asked.

VIRGINIA moves on. VANESSA stops a second, briefly shocked. They are heading towards VANESSA'S three children who are gathered in a group near the bushes round something not yet seen. JULIAN BELL is 15, sturdy and muscular ; QUENTIN BELL is 13, looking like a young soldier ; and **ANGELICA GARNETT** is an exceptionally beautiful little girl of 5.

> VANESSA

Hello changelings, what have you got? What have you found?

> JULIAN

We've found a bird.

> VANESSA

Did you? Where did you find that?

> JULIAN

I think it must have fallen from the tree.

QUENTIN holds a dying thrush out in his hands, a bundle of gray feathers.

> VANESSA

Goodness, just look at him.

> QUENTIN

He's alive. I think we might be able to save him.

> VANESSA

Save him?

VANESSA frowns.

> VANESSA

I think you have to be careful, Quentin. There's a time to die.
It may be the bird's time.

Fearing such talk may upset her, **VANESSA** instinctively squeezes **VIRGINIA'S** hand.

JULIAN

Come on, let's pick some grass. Let's pick some grass to make a grave.

VANESSA is about to protest, but JULIAN interrupts.

JULIAN

I'm just saying: then at least there'll be a bed for him to die on.

QUENTIN

Come on, Nessa, let's make a grave.

VANESSA

Oh God, oh very well. I'm coming. Wait for me, then.

VANESSA runs off with the boys.

42. EXT. HOGARTH HOUSE. GARDEN.
     DAY.

ANGELICA is making the little bed of twigs. The others have gone off to pick grass. VIRGINIA appears above ANGELICA with some yellow roses.

VIRGINIA

Do you think she'd like roses?

ANGELICA

Yes.

VIRGINIA

Let's put roses round the grass.

VIRGINIA kneels down next to ANGELICA and helps her arrange the little bed. The bird is lying to one side. In the distance the boys are calling "Mother. There's some good stuff over here. Mother! Mother!"

ANGELICA

Is it a she?

VIRGINIA

Yes. The females are larger and less colorful.

The sticks, grass and leaves are now laid out in a rough circle. ANGELICA'S hands have the dead bird protected inside them as she lays down the thrush, arranging her feet under her. ANGELICA and VIRGINIA decorate the circle of leaves with roses.

ANGELICA

What happens when we die?

VIRGINIA

What happens? We return to the place we came from.

ANGELICA

I don't remember where I came from.

VIRGINIA

Nor do I.

ANGELICA frowns, trying to understand.

ANGELICA

She looks very small.

VIRGINIA

Yes. That's one of the things that happens. We look smaller.

ANGELICA

But very peaceful.

VIRGINIA smiles at ANGELICA. Suddenly VANESSA arrives with the boys, her energy breaking up the moment of quiet.

VANESSA

Is it done? Have we finished? Is the bird-funeral complete?
Have bird-obsequies been done?

VIRGINIA

They have.

VANESSA

Good. Very well then. Are we to be denied tea altogether for
coming so early?

ANGELICA runs off, happy at the job done. But VIRGINIA doesn't yet
move.

VIRGINIA

No. Of course not.

VANESSA

Well, then.

VANESSA says "Come on, boys" and walks off up the lawn with JULIAN
and QUENTIN. They are all chattering as they go, JULIAN asking
"Where's Nelly gone?", VANESSA replying "She had to go to London to
get ginger" JULIAN: "Did that make her angry?" VANESSA: "Virginia
says very". QUENTIN: "I like it when Nelly gets angry. It's funny." Then
it's silent. VIRGINIA is left alone. She has not moved. She is still looking
at the bird's grave. The bird is perfectly at peace and surrounded with
petals. VIRGINIA looks. Slowly, VIRGINIA closes her eyes. Her face
becomes a death-mask.

43. INT. BROWNS' HOUSE. BEDROOM.
    DAY.

1951. LAURA is lain out on the bed, an identical look on her face to
VIRGINIA'S. Then, impulsively, she gets up from the bed.

44. INT. BROWNS' HOUSE. LIVING ROOM.
DAY.

RICHIE is sitting by himself playing on the carpet with his toys. He looks up, missing nothing, as LAURA comes out of the bedroom. She smiles absently at him, and walks across the living room to pick up the tapestry bag which is lying on a chair. She takes it with her and goes into the bathroom.

45. INT. BROWN'S HOUSE. BATHROOM.
DAY.

LAURA opens the mirrored cupboard above the sink. In it, there are a few odd bottles of aspirin, etc. She reaches for some bottles of prescribed sleeping pills. She opens the tapestry bag, puts the bottles inside and goes out.

46. INT. BROWNS' HOUSE. LIVING ROOM.
DAY.

LAURA comes out of the bedroom with the tapestry bag. RICHIE looks up again, trying to puzzle out where she has been. LAURA heads straight for the kitchen, where she puts the bag on a high surface, out of the child's reach. LAURA reaches once more for the flour and eggs.

LAURA

Hey, bug, I've got this idea. We're going to make another cake. We're going to make a better one.

RICHIE

What happened to the first one?

LAURA smiles at him as if everything were completely normal.

LAURA

Then after that, I think we should go out.

47. EXT. CLARISSA'S APARTMENT.
DAY.

2001. At once a man's finger pressing the intercom. LOUIS WATERS is leonine, silvery, handsome in his late 40s, casually but perfectly dressed: a once-startlingly good-looking man, now a little faded. He is nervous. It's taken him an effort to ring the bell. After a moment he hears CLARISSA'S voice.

CLARISSA'S VOICE

Yes?

LOUIS

Clarissa, it's Louis. Louis Waters.

CLARISSA

Louis? My God. You're early.

LOUIS

Do you mind? Is it all right?

48. INT. CLARISSA'S APARTMENT. VESTIBULE.
DAY.

CLARISSA has pressed the buzzer and LOUIS is coming into the vestibule of the building. As he does CLARISSA swings open the door of the apartment to greet him. She has an apron around her waist and green plastic gloves on. Her hair is a mess and LOUIS has plainly interrupted her in mid-work. She is listening to a CD, which is booming out behind her.

CLARISSA

Why should I mind? I'm delighted.

LOUIS

Well now.

They fall into each other's arms, embracing. They hold each other some time, with real need. Then CLARISSA lets go and sees that LOUIS'S eyes are moist.

LOUIS

I feel I'm interrupting.

CLARISSA

Why, no.

LOUIS

I know the ceremony's not till five, but I flew in this morning.

CLARISSA stands a moment, shaking her head.

CLARISSA

Richard's going to be thrilled. He'll be thrilled to see you.

LOUIS

You think so?

CLARISSA

Of course. Of course he will.

There's just a moment's hesitation.

CLARISSA

What are we doing? We should go in.

49. INT. APARTMENT.
DAY.

CLARISSA leads LOUIS into the apartment, taking off her apron. LOUIS follows her, hesitant, wondering what is wrong beyond her astonishment at seeing him again.

LOUIS

Are you all right?

CLARISSA

Oh, sure. It's nothing. It's just the party.

LOUIS

Oh, right.

LOUIS looks around the room. Everything is now cleared to the sides. There are bunches of flowers everywhere. Yellow roses abound. CLARISSA turns off the CD of Jessye Norman singing one of Strauss's last songs.

LOUIS

Wow. It's looking beautiful. Are you still with . . .

CLARISSA

Yes. I'm still with her. Yes. Ten years. It's crazy.

LOUIS

Why is it crazy?

CLARISSA shakes her head, embarrassed.

CLARISSA

No reason. Would you like a drink?

LOUIS

Some water.

CLARISSA

OK.

50. INT. APARTMENT. KITCHEN.
    DAY.

CLARISSA lifts the lid on the big pot of shellfish, which is now bubbling on the stove. Around the kitchen, the ingredients to make crab soufflé roll are laid out. CLARISSA takes a look, then takes off her plastic gloves, fills glasses with ice and carbonated water. She looks through from the kitchen to where LOUIS is standing alone, still admiring the apartment.

                         LOUIS

And you're still an editor?

                         CLARISSA

Oh, sure.

                         LOUIS

Still with the same publisher?

CLARISSA nods.

                         CLARISSA

How's San Francisco?

                         LOUIS

Oh. It's one of those cities people *tell* you to like.

LOUIS stops a moment looking a framed photograph of the young RICHARD, looking handsome, healthy and young.

                         CLARISSA

Richard said he thought you were happy out there.

                         LOUIS

Oh great. So now the illness makes him psychic?

CLARISSA hands him his water.

CLARISSA

Louis, you have to prepare yourself. He's very changed.

LOUIS has picked out a copy of Richard's book from CLARISSA'S shelves. CLARISSA goes back to her cooking.

LOUIS

I read the book . . .

CLARISSA

Oh, God!

LOUIS

Exactly. I thought you were meant to do more than just change peoples' names.

CLARISSA

Well . . .

LOUIS

Isn't it meant to be fiction? He even had you living on Tenth Street.

CLARISSA frowns, not liking the way the conversation is going.

CLARISSA

It isn't me.

LOUIS

Isn't it?

CLARISSA

You know how Richard is. It's a fantasy.

LOUIS

A whole chapter about "Should she buy some nail polish?" And then guess what? After fifty pages *she doesn't*!

CLARISSA smiles, but LOUIS isn't amused.

LOUIS

The whole thing seems to go on for eternity. Nothing happens. Then wham! For no reason she kills herself.

CLARISSA

His mother kills herself.

LOUIS

Yeah. Sure. His mother. But still for no reason.

CLARISSA

Well . . .

LOUIS

Out of the blue.

LOUIS seems annoyed, but CLARISSA speaks quietly, trying to reach him now.

CLARISSA

I know the book's tough. But I liked it. I know. Only one thing upset me.

LOUIS

Oh yeah? What was that? What upset you?

LOUIS is looking at her warily now, as if he feared being hurt.

CLARISSA

Well . . . that there wasn't more about you.

LOUIS

That's kind.

LOUIS looks up, caught off balance. Now he is moved, and risks a confidence.

LOUIS

I went back to Wellfleet.

CLARISSA

You did?

LOUIS

One day. I didn't tell you.

CLARISSA

No. But then I never see you.

LOUIS

You remember the house?

LOUIS stops, thinking.

CLARISSA

I think you're courageous.

LOUIS

Courageous? Why?

CLARISSA

To dare to go visit.

LOUIS frowns.

CLARISSA

What I mean is: to face the fact we've lost those feelings for
ever.

CLARISSA'S eyes are full of tears, and she seems to have forgotten LOUIS
is there.

CLARISSA

Shit.

Clarissa . . .

CLARISSA

I don't know what's happening. I'm sorry. I seem to be in some
strange sort of mood. I seem to be unraveling . . .

LOUIS

Clarissa, I shouldn't have come.

CLARISSA holds out a hand to stop him coming over to comfort her.

CLARISSA

No, it's not you. Really. It's more . . . it's like having a presentiment. Do you know what I'm saying?

CLARISSA wipes her eyes, tries to make light of it.

CLARISSA

Oh, God, it's probably just nerves about the party. Bad hostess.

Suddenly CLARISSA sinks to the floor, not able to control herself anymore.

LOUIS

Clarissa, what's happening?

CLARISSA

Jesus!

LOUIS

What is it?

CLARISSA has gone away to the wall, like a child, sobbing now, with her
hand raised to hide her face.

CLARISSA

Oh, God!

LOUIS

Do you want me to go?

CLARISSA tries desperately to turn her grief to anger.

CLARISSA

No. Don't go. Explain to me! Why is this happening?

LOUIS moves towards her to try and reassure her by taking her in his arms.

CLARISSA

No. Don't touch me. It's better you don't.

LOUIS stands useless. CLARISSA looks at him a moment through her tears. Then she tries desperately.

CLARISSA

It's too much. It's just too much. You fly in from San Francisco. I've been nursing Richard for years . . .

LOUIS

I know.

CLARISSA

And all that time I've held myself together . . . no problem . . .

There's a silence. Neither of them can say anything. CLARISSA just looks pleadingly at him from the floor.

LOUIS

Yes.

Neither speaks. CLARISSA wipes her tears with her sleeve. She's quiet when she talks.

CLARISSA

One morning. In Wellfleet. I'd been sleeping with him and I

was on the back porch. He came out. He put his hand on my shoulder. "Good morning, Mrs. Dalloway."

CLARISSA is lost a moment in the memory.

CLARISSA

And ever since then, I've been stuck.

LOUIS

Stuck?

CLARISSA

I mean, with the name.

There's a silence. Then CLARISSA gestures towards LOUIS, to divert.

CLARISSA

And now you walk in . . . to see you walk in. Because I never see you. Look at you!

LOUIS looks at her, wanting to help.

CLARISSA

Anyway, it doesn't matter. It was you he stayed with. It was you he lived with. You'll see when he comes. He's still Richard. His mind wanders and he's in a lot of pain. But there's some constant quality. There's his Richard-ness.

LOUIS moves towards her, careful about what he wants to spell out.

LOUIS

The day I left him I got on a train and made my way across Europe. I felt free for the first time in years.

There is a silence. CLARISSA stares, taking in what LOUIS has just said. Then she gets up, trying to get back to normal.

CLARISSA

So. You must tell me about San Francisco.

LOUIS

What's to tell? I still teach drama to idiots. Mostly.

CLARISSA

They can't all be idiots.

LOUIS

No.

LOUIS has put his glass down.

LOUIS

No, in fact . . . I shouldn't tell you this: I've fallen in love.

CLARISSA

Really?

LOUIS

Yes. With a student.

CLARISSA

A student?

LOUIS

Exactly.

LOUIS acknowledges the absurdity of it.

LOUIS

I know. You think "Am I still up for this? All this inten-
sity . . ." All those arguments, doors being slammed . . . well,
you know what it's like . . .

CLARISSA says nothing.

LOUIS

Are you feeling better?

CLARISSA

A little. Thank you.

CLARISSA goes to the sink. LOUIS is suddenly embarrassed.

LOUIS

Do you think I'm ridiculous?

CLARISSA

Ridiculous. Fortunate, too.

51. INT. BROWNS' HOUSE.
    DAY.

1951. LAURA takes a second cake out of the oven and sets it down on a cake-rack. She looks at it a moment. It is much better than the first. It reads HAPPY BIRTHDAY DAN and is fringed with yellow roses. LAURA takes off her oven gloves and reaches for the tapestry bag. She goes out.

52. INT. CAR.
    DAY.

The tapestry bag lands with a wham! on the back seat of the car. LAURA then bundles a rather surprised-looking RICHIE into the passenger seat. Then LAURA goes round and gets in the driver's side.

LAURA

I'm going to leave you at Mrs. Latch's. I have to do something.

LAURA is dressed and made-up, armored to go out into the world. RICHIE is looking at her as she starts the car.

RICHIE

Mommy, I don't want to go.

LAURA

You have to. I'm sorry. I have to do something before Daddy
comes home.

They drive off down the suburban street, fringed with palm trees.

53. EXT. MRS. LATCH'S HOUSE.
    DAY.

A cute suburban house with plaster squirrels on the gable over the garage.
MRS. LATCH, a big, florid woman in Bermuda shorts, opens the door.
RICHIE is holding LAURA'S hand, and looking very reluctant to go in
to the house.

MRS. LATCH

Hello.

LAURA

Hi, Mrs. Latch. My boy's not very happy.

RICHIE

Mommy, I don't want to do this.

LAURA

I have to go, honey.

LAURA stoops down to his level and kisses him.

MRS. LATCH

Your mommy has things she must do. If you come in, I got
cookies.

LAURA takes him so that she can look him directly in the eye.

73

LAURA

Baby. Baby, you have to be brave now.

MRS. LATCH

Don't you worry, he's going to be fine.

MRS. LATCH reaches out and takes RICHIE'S hand. Turned away now from her son, LAURA walks across the lawn back to the car. Without warning, her face crumples in tears, but as she reaches the car she wipes her eyes with her hand to hide her distress. Then she turns back to wave.

LAURA

Honey!

RICHIE waves back from the step. LAURA quickly gets into the car, grinning at him. She can barely get the key in the starter, but when she does, she turns and drives away.

54. INT & EXT. LAURA'S CAR. LOS ANGELES.
    DAY.

LAURA is beginning to drive away down the road. She looks nervously in the rear-view mirror. She sees RICHIE run out of MRS LATCH'S arms and into the road screaming desperately.

RICHIE

Mommy! Mommy! No!

LAURA swings the wheel decisively to the left and with a little squeal of rubber, accelerates away. RICHIE stands alone in the middle of the street.

55. INT AND EXT. LAURA'S CAR.
    DAY.

Now LAURA is cruising on a Los Angeles freeway. For a moment, her higher speed and the freedom of the road gives the feeling that she has successfully escaped.

56. INT. MRS. LATCH'S HOUSE.
DAY.

Back in the living room of Mrs. Latch's house, RICHIE moodily gets out a building set and begins building a small house. MRS LATCH watches from the doorway.

57. INT. LAURA'S CAR.
DAY.

LAURA drives intently. She is aimless, distressed. But then she looks to the side of the freeway where there is a sign for the *Normandy Hotel*. Impulsively, with no pre-planning, LAURA swings the car dangerously across lanes and takes it out along the slipway towards the hotel.

58. INT. MRS LATCH'S HOUSE.
DAY.

RICHIE has finished the little house. Now he picks up the completed building and tumbles it bad-temperedly back into the box.

59. EXT. NORMANDY HOTEL. LOS ANGELES.
DAY.

LAURA walks towards a huge wedding-cake hotel, a pseudo-Spanish 50s palace. She carries no luggage except her tapestry bag.

60. INT. NORMANDY HOTEL. ROOM.
DAY.

LAURA has checked in to the hotel and is now standing in the room she has reserved. It is featureless, anonymous—green spreads and candy wallpaper. LAURA is dropping fifty cents into a HOTEL CLERK'S outstretched hand.

CLERK

Breakfast is served between seven and eleven in the Regency Room. There's a swimming pool at the back, and the hotel is open for twenty-four hours.

He pockets his tip.

CLERK

Thank you, ma'am. Is there anything else you need?

LAURA hesitates a moment.

LAURA

Yes. No. Not to be disturbed.

He goes out. LAURA is left alone. She looks round the room. There is a moment of silence, of relief. LAURA looks round, not quite knowing what to do next.

LAURA sits on the edge of the bed and opens her bag. She takes out the pale green toilet bag and unzips it. She takes the little rank of pill bottles out and sets them down on the bed cover. As she does so, she sees her copy of *Mrs. Dalloway* at the bottom of the tapestry bag.

61. INT. NORMANDY HOTEL.
DAY.

A few minutes later. Now LAURA is stretched out reading on the bed, a pillow against her back. As LAURA reads her book, the text is heard in VIRGINIA'S voice.

                              VIRGINIA (*v.o.*)

Did it matter, then, she asked herself, walking towards Bond
Street, did it matter that she must inevitably cease completely . . .

LAURA pulls her blouse out from her skirt to loosen it, and puts her
hand on her pregnant stomach.

                              VIRGINIA (*v.o.*)

All this must go on without her ; did she resent it ; or did it
not become consoling to believe that death ended absolutely?

LAURA rubs her naked stomach slightly, feeling the child within.

                              VIRGINIA (*v.o.*)

It is possible to die.

Suddenly brackish water floods from underneath, washing up over the
sides of the bed. LAURA, in her imagination, sinks under the water,
strewn with weeds, and then drowns.

62. INT. HOGARTH HOUSE. DRAWING ROOM.
     DAY.

1923. VIRGINIA is sitting with VANESSA having tea. JULIAN and
QUENTIN are at the other end of the room. VIRGINIA is completely
lost in her own thoughts.

                              VIRGINIA (*v.o.*)

It is possible to die.

VIRGINIA turns her head and becomes aware that VANESSA has been
speaking. She only hears the end of what has obviously been a long dis-
course.

. . . there was a lovely coat for Angelica at Harrods, but then nothing for the boys and it seemed so unfair. Why should Angelica be favored?

VIRGINIA does not reply.

VANESSA

Virginia? Virginia? What are you thinking about?

VIRGINIA is still looking at her a little blankly. JULIAN and QUENTIN are nudging each other, laughing at how odd VIRGINIA is. ANGELICA runs across to VIRGINIA, who scoops her up and puts her on her knee.

VANESSA

Your aunt's a very lucky woman, Angelica, because she has two lives. Most of us have only one. But she has the life she leads and she also has the book she's writing. This makes her very fortunate indeed.

VIRGINIA smiles at ANGELICA on her knee.

ANGELICA

What were you thinking about?

VIRGINIA

Oh. I was going to kill my heroine. But I've changed my mind.

63. INT. NORMANDY HOTEL. ROOM.
    DAY.

1951. Back in the (dry) bedroom, LAURA is lying on the bed, the pills still visible on the table beside her. She still has the book in front of her, but she is not reading it. She puts it to one side. Then she rubs her naked stomach again. Her eyes fill with tears.

LAURA

I can't! I can't!

64. INT. HOGARTH HOUSE. DRAWING ROOM.
    DAY.

1923. VIRGINIA is just as before.

VIRGINIA
I fear I may have to kill someone else instead.

65. INT. HOGARTH HOUSE. HALL.
    DAY.

Everyone is now gathered in the hall, saying good-bye. There is a car wait-ing outside which is being loaded. QUENTIN, JULIAN and ANGELICA are all in front as VANESSA and VIRGINIA make their way to the door.

VANESSA
It was a fascinating visit. They enjoyed it thoroughly.

VIRGINIA
Do you have to go already? I do wish you wouldn't go.

VANESSA
Why, Virginia, the last thing you need is our noisiness. My hopeless, clumsy boys.

VANESSA smiles at the lads.

VANESSA
Say good-bye, boys.

VIRGINIA
Good-bye, children.

The boys say "Good-bye" and "Good-bye, Aunt" and shake VIRGINIA'S hand. They go out of the front door towards a waiting taxi. VIRGINIA turns to her sister.

VIRGINIA

And you will return to what? To concerts? To parties?

VANESSA

Tonight? An insufferable dinner which not even you could envy, Virginia.

VIRGINIA

But I do.

Suddenly she looks VANESSA in the eye.

VIRGINIA

Kiss me.

It starts as a formal kiss, but then VIRGINIA, shockingly direct, pushes her lips against VANESSA'S. VIRGINIA holds her mouth a moment. When they part, VANESSA is overwhelmed, blushing at the power of VIRGINIA'S need.

VIRGINIA

Did you think I was better? Say something, Nessa. Didn't you think I seemed better?

VANESSA

Yes, Virginia. You seem better.

VIRGINIA continues to look at her sister, pleadingly.

VIRGINIA

You think . . . you think I may one day escape?

There is a silence, the two women still eye to eye.

VANESSA

One day. One.

VIRGINIA

Nessa . . .

There's a short silence, broken by the sound of a car horn outside.

VANESSA

Come, Angelica. We must go.

VANESSA and ANGELICA go out of the door. ANGELICA turns back and waves.

ANGELICA

Good-bye.

VIRGINIA

Good-bye, little girl.

NELLIE, returning from outside, closes the door and gives VIRGINIA a look as she returns to the kitchen. VIRGINIA stands alone in the hall.

LEONARD is standing at the end of the corridor, watching.

66. EXT. HOGARTH HOUSE.
     DAY.

The boys are already in the taxi. VANESSA, obviously upset, wordlessly ushers ANGELICA to get in. Then she gets in herself, and draws ANGELICA to her.

VANESSA

Here. On my knee. Stay close.

VANESSA signals to the DRIVER.

Driver.

67. EXT. CLARISSA'S APARTMENT.
DAY.

2001. LOUIS lets the outside door of CLARISSA'S apartment building close behind him. He stands a moment at the top of the steps, full of relief to have left. Then, gratefully, he goes on his way.

68. INT. CLARISSA'S APARTMENT.
DAY.

CLARISSA closes the door of the apartment and goes back into her living room, intending to resume her preparations for the party. But instead she stands, in the middle of the room, now bereft. She does not move.

69. INT. HOGARTH HOUSE.
DAY.

1923. VIRGINIA walks alone up the staircase. At the half-way landing there is a large window. VIRGINIA stops. Outside, she can see the happy family departing—the three children chattering excitedly to VANESSA. Their car disappears. VIRGINIA watches.

70. EXT. TENTH STREET.
DAY.

2001. A handsome, 19 year-old GIRL, lush and strong, in combat trousers and sweater comes along Tenth Street. She crackles with health like an Irish farm-girl. She bounds up the steps of CLARISSA'S apartment block and lets herself in with her key.

71. INT. CLARISSA'S APARTMENT.
    DAY.

The girl is CLARISSA'S daughter JULIA and now she is letting herself in
to the apartment.

                    JULIA
I'm sorry, I know, I tried to get here earlier. I tried. OK? Don't
start. I know. It's just incredibly important. Because it's your
party.

CLARISSA turns from where she is standing.

                    CLARISSA
Julia. How you've been doing?

                    JULIA
I'm fine.

CLARISSA has gone over to embrace her.

                    CLARISSA
Come here. *What've* you been doing?

                    JULIA
Well, studying, Mom.

JULIA eases out of her mother's needy embrace, blithely to take off her
backpack.

                    JULIA
What should I do? Chairs?

                    CLARISSA
Oh. Can you clear my desk?

CLARISSA'S desk is covered in books which JULIA now clears by carrying them through to the bedroom. As she goes she calls back to her mother.

JULIA

I bumped into Louis Waters.

CLARISSA

You did. Where?

JULIA

In the street. They're all here aren't they? The ghosts. The ghosts are assembling for the party. He's weird.

JULIA on her way through sees her mother's face.

JULIA

You mean you can't see that? You can't see Louis Waters is weird?

CLARISSA

I can see that he's sad.

JULIA

All your friends are sad.

JULIA expects CLARISSA to laugh, but then stops, books in hand, seeing how preoccupied her mother is.

JULIA

You've been crying. What's happening?

CLARISSA

All it is: I looked around this room. I thought, I'm giving a party. All I want to do is just give a party.

JULIA

And?

CLARISSA shakes her head, angry with herself.

CLARISSA

I know why he does it! He does it deliberately!

JULIA

Who? Is this Richard?

CLARISSA

Of course!

JULIA smiles to herself, as if she's used to it.

CLARISSA

He looks at me. He did it this morning. He gave me that look.

JULIA

What look?

CLARISSA

Oh, to say: "You're trivial, your life is so *trivial*. Daily stuff, schedules. Parties. Details."

CLARISSA turns, suddenly protesting.

CLARISSA

That's what he means by it. That's what he's saying!

JULIA

Mom, it only matters if you think it's true.

CLARISSA looks at her, taken aback by what JULIA has said. They both become quiet now.

JULIA

Well? Do you? Tell me.

There's a silence.

CLARISSA

When I'm with him, then, yes, I'm living. That's what I feel.
And when I'm not, yes, things seem kind of silly.

JULIA walks away to the bedroom, struck by her mother's tactlessness.

CLARISSA

I don't mean with you. Never with you. But the rest of it.

JULIA

Sally?

CLARISSA

The rest of it.

CLARISSA has followed JULIA into the bedroom and now they lie down,
side by side, on the bed.

CLARISSA

If you say to me: when was I happiest?

JULIA

Mom . . .

CLARISSA

Tell me the moment you were happiest . . .

JULIA

I know. It was years ago.

CLARISSA

Yes.

JULIA

All you're saying is, you were once young.

CLARISSA smiles at JULIA'S remark. But JULIA knows it is still not resolved.

> CLARISSA
>
> I remember one morning. Getting up at dawn. There was such a sense of possibility. We were going to do everything. Do you know that feeling?

JULIA nods, finally allowing what her mother is saying.

> CLARISSA
>
> I remember thinking: 'This is the beginning of happiness'. That's what I thought. 'So this is the feeling. This is where it starts. And of course there'll always be more.' It never occurred to me: it wasn't the beginning. It *was* happiness. It was the moment, right then.

There is a silence. JULIA looks thoughtfully at her mother. Then the door buzzer sounds. CLARISSA goes to the intercom, and a VOICE calls through: "Caterers."

71. INT. HOGARTH HOUSE. KITCHEN.
    EVE.

Beef being dumped down into a frying pan filled with onions and being vigorously stirred, a pan of beef bones bubbling next to it. NELLY and LOTTIE working together in the well-lit kitchen, a whole range of vegetables laid out on the chopping boards for supper.

NELLY, who misses nothing, looks up from her cooking at the sound of someone coming downstairs. The kitchen door is open and gives onto the stairway. A figure moves quickly by, but NELLY sees. VIRGINIA is heading out in a long coat. LOTTIE has also looked up, the two of them noting VIRGINIA'S departure.

72. EXT. HOGARTH HOUSE.
    EVE.

VIRGINIA in her coat hurrying out, trying to make sure she is not noticed. She moves quickly through the garden. In the distance, LEONARD is digging at the edge of the garden. But his back is turned and he does not notice her. She hastens towards the gate, and out into the road outside.

73. EXT. RICHMOND STATION.
    EVE.

It is a summer evening, darkening a little, as VIRGINIA comes to the Victorian portico of Richmond station. Two MEN, returning from London, pass, and she catches a whiff of their conversation: "I told him that's what he had to do and if he didn't like it that was his business." VIRGINIA passes them, trying not to be noticed, going into the hall, a fine canopied space of glass and arched ironwork. She goes to the ticket booth.

VIRGINIA

I need a ticket to London, please.

CLERK

Yes, Madam. A single or a return?

74. INT. HOGARTH HOUSE.
    EVE.

In a presentiment of what will happen again in 18 years' time LEONARD WOOLF comes in from the garden. It's a different house and a different hallway, but the action is the same. LEONARD sits to put on his slippers, hearing the sounds of the house. Then, as if noticing something, frowns.

75. INT. HOGARTH HOUSE. KITCHEN.
    EVE.

LEONARD appears at the kitchen door. NELLY is standing behind her stew.

> LEONARD

Ah, Nelly, good evening. I was wondering if you'd seen Mrs. Woolf.

> NELLY

I thought you knew, sir. Mrs. Woolf has gone out.

76. EXT. HOGARTH HOUSE. GARDEN. EVE.

LEONARD WOOLF, in blind panic, fleeing the house, not in a coat, just out into the garden, and away off down the road.

77. EXT. PARADISE ROAD.
EVE.

A middle-aged man, LEONARD WOOLF, running in his slippers, vest and corduroy jacket, charging down the hill towards the town.

78. EXT. RICHMOND STATION. PLATFORM.
EVE.

LEONARD comes down the steps towards the railway platform. He sees VIRGINIA sitting rather conspicuously by herself on a bench at the end of the platform. A train has just gone, so there is not another traveler in sight. The railway line stretches away to London, empty and quiet. VIRGINIA is trying not to be self-conscious, but she is tense. She turns.

> VIRGINIA

Ah Mr. Woolf, what an unexpected pleasure.

> LEONARD

And perhaps you could tell me what you think you're doing.

What I was doing? Why—

I went to look for you and you weren't there.

LEONARD moves towards her. VIRGINIA stays calm, resisting his panic.

You were working in the garden. I didn't wish to disturb you.

You disturb me when you disappear.

I didn't disappear. I went for a walk.

Is that all?

VIRGINIA doesn't answer.

Is that all? Just a walk?

They have neither of them moved. LEONARD is firm now.

Virginia, Nelly is cooking dinner. She has already had a difficult day. We must go home. We must eat Nelly's dinner. It is our obligation to eat Nelly's dinner.

There is no such obligation! No such obligation exists.

Virginia, you have an obligation to your own sanity.

And what is your role, Leonard? My husband? Or my prison guard?

LEONARD is shocked by her fierceness. He tries to soften his tone, but VIRGINIA flares up as soon as he speaks.

LEONARD

Virginia . . .

VIRGINIA

I have endured this custody. I have endured this imprisonment. I am attended by doctors. Everywhere I am attended by doctors who inform me of my own interests.

LEONARD

They know your interests.

VIRGINIA

They do not! They do not speak for my interests! How dare they presume? Let us imagine a life in which women are the doctors, and the men sit alone all day in shuttered rooms in the suburbs. Let us imagine that!

LEONARD shifts, but is still determined not to back down. Behind him the odd PASSENGER is beginning to arrive to wait for London train.

LEONARD

Virginia, it is hard . . . I can see it must be hard for a woman . . . for a woman of your . . .

VIRGINIA

Of what? A woman of my what exactly?

LEONARD

A woman of your gifts . . .

VIRGINIA

Oh I see . . .

LEONARD

. . . of your . . . of your talents . . . to accept that she is not always the best judge of her own condition.

VIRGINIA

No? Who, then, is a better judge? Bring this judge to Platform One. Let me meet them.

VIRGINIA is looking at him defiantly.

LEONARD

You have a history . . .

VIRGINIA

Oh yes . . .

LEONARD

You came to Richmond with a history of confinement. Fits. Blackouts. Moods. Hearing voices. We brought you here to escape the irrevocable damage you intended to yourself. Twice you have tried to take your life by your own hand.

VIRGINIA is watching him closely now, attending every word, still not giving way.

LEONARD

I live daily with that threat.

VIRGINIA looks at him, refusing to answer.

LEONARD

I set up the press, *we* set up the printing press . . .

VIRGINIA

Yes . . .

LEONARD

Not for itself. Not purely as a thing in itself. But that you
might find a ready occupation, a ready source of absorption
and of remedy.

VIRGINIA

Like needlework?

VIRGINIA has suddenly shouted. LEONARD for a moment loses his
temper.

LEONARD

It was done for you! It was done for your betterment! It was
done out of love. If I did not know you better I would call this
ingratitude.

VIRGINIA

I am ungrateful? You call me ungrateful?

VIRGINIA looks at him, accusing, shaking.

VIRGINIA

My life has been stolen from me. I am living in a town I have
no wish to live in. I am living a life I have no wish to live. And
I am asking how this has occurred.

VIRGINIA nods, sure of her point. There are now several PASSENGERS
on the long London platform, but VIRGINIA and LEONARD ignore
them completely.

VIRGINIA

It is time for us to move back to London. I miss London. I
miss London life.

LEONARD

This is not you speaking, Virginia. This is an aspect of your illness.

VIRGINIA

It is me. It is my voice. It is mine and mine alone.

LEONARD

It is not your voice. It is only a voice you hear.

VIRGINIA

It is not! It is mine! I am dying in this town!

VIRGINIA is inflamed, passionate, almost mad. LEONARD looks at her, trying to keep calm.

LEONARD

If you were clear . . . if you were thinking clearly, you would remember: it was London which brought you low.

VIRGINIA

If I were thinking clearly?

LEONARD

We brought you to Richmond to give you peace.

VIRGINIA takes a moment to summon all her lucidity.

VIRGINIA

If I were thinking clearly? If I were thinking clearly, Leonard, I would tell you that I wrestle alone in the dark, in the deep dark, and that only I can know, only I can understand my own condition. You live with the threat, you tell me. You live with the threat of my extinction.

There is a silence. She is trembling, white.

Leonard, I live with it too.

Now it is LEONARD who cannot answer.

This is my right. This is the right of every human being. I choose not the suffocating anesthetic of the suburbs, but the violent jolt of the capital. That is my choice. The meanest patient, yes even the very lowest, is allowed some say in the matter of her own prescription. Thereby she defines her humanity.

VIRGINIA is calm now, certain.

I wish for your sake, Leonard, that I could be happy in this quietness. But if it is a choice between Richmond and death, I choose death.

There are tears now in LEONARD'S eyes.

Very well. London, then. We shall go back to London.

LEONARD bows his head, overwhelmed by the defeat of his strategy. There is a silence. VIRGINIA watches, full of feeling for him. Then, at the opposite platform the train from London arrives. From its doors, phalanxes of COMMUTERS in dark coats and hats get down onto the platform and head for the exit. LEONARD looks up, wiping away his tears.

You must be hungry. I am a little hungry myself.

VIRGINIA smiles. They look at each other, the issue at last resolved between them.

Come along.

VIRGINIA and LEONARD get up and walk together along the deserted platform, both shaken by the encounter. After a moment, VIRGINIA takes his arm. They walk a while, arm in arm, merging into the crowd of COMMUTERS. Then VIRGINIA speaks, almost as an afterthought.

VIRGINIA

You do not find peace by avoiding life, Leonard.

79. EXT/INT. MRS. LATCH'S HOUSE. LOS ANGELES.
     EVE.

1951. LAURA'S car draws up outside MRS. LATCH'S house. RICHIE has plainly heard her arrive, for when she looks to the window, RICHIE is already banging his hands against it and screaming "Mommy! Mommy!" LAURA looks, fearful. Then she gets out of the car. Along the neat suburban street, sprinklers play across lawns, catching the evening light like fountains. RICHIE comes running from the house towards his mother with a triumphant cry of "It's Mommy!" MRS. LATCH follows.

MRS. LATCH

Why, hello, Laura.

LAURA

Oh, Mrs. Latch. I'm sorry I'm late.

LAURA picks RICHIE up and he buries his face in her shoulder.

LAURA

Oh, now. Hey. Hey. Hey there, bug. What's wrong? What's wrong?

MRS. LATCH smiles reassuringly.

MRS. LATCH

He's fine. He's been fine. He's just pleased to see you.

LAURA

Come on, it wasn't that bad. It wasn't that bad, was it?

RICHIE has buried himself in LAURA. MRS. LATCH nods at LAURA'S hair.

MRS. LATCH

You got it cut, then?

LAURA

Oh, yes. Yes. No problem.

MRS. LATCH

It looks great.

LAURA

Thank you. They didn't have to do very much.

LAURA smiles, embarrassed at the lie.

MRS. LATCH

We had a fine time together.

LAURA

Thank you. Very much.

80. EXT/INT. CAR.
EVE.

The two of them are driving side by side. LAURA has her eyes on the road. RICHIE is staring straight ahead, not looking at her. The car is moving noiselessly along suburban avenues. There is a long silence. They seem more like two adults than mother and child.

LAURA

So that wasn't too bad, was it? I wasn't gone long.

RICHIE

No, you weren't long.

LAURA

That's right. At one point . . . I don't know . . . there was a moment when I thought I might be longer. But I changed my mind.

RICHIE says nothing.

LAURA

Honey, what is it?

RICHIE

Mommy, I love you.

There is a moment's pause.

LAURA

I love you too, baby.

There is a thoughtful look on RICHIE'S face.

LAURA

What's wrong?

RICHIE looks at LAURA as if he knows where she has been.

LAURA

What?

But still RICHIE says nothing, just goes on looking.

LAURA

Don't worry, honey. Everything's fine. We're going to have a
wonderful party. We've made Daddy such a nice cake.

RICHIE is still looking at her, watchful.

LAURA

I love you, sweetheart. You're my guy.

RICHIE is seen from LAURA'S point of view, his little face flushed for a
moment with pleasure. The sound fades, and there is a slow dissolve
through to :

81. INT. RICHARD'S APARTMENT.
     EVE.

2001. RICHARD'S face seen from the exact same point of view. The child
has become the man. RICHARD is sitting in the near dark, a gleam of
light catching the sweat on his forehead. He has not moved from his
chair, nor has he dressed. He sits thinking back to the scene in the car.
LAURA'S voice is heard in RICHARD'S head.

LAURA (*v.o.*)

I love you, sweetheart. You're my guy.

82. EXT/INT. TRIANGLE BUILDING.
     EVE.

CLARISSA gets out of a hired car in the afternoon light, and heads into
the doorway of the triangle building. She gets quickly into the elevator.
The elevator ascends.

83. INT. RICHARD'S APARTMENT.
     EVE.

Beside RICHARD, a photograph of his mother, LAURA, on her wedding day, eyes down. RICHARD looks at it, the extreme sweat of illness running down his face.

84. INT. RICHARD'S APARTMENT.
     EVE.

CLARISSA, in a repeat of the morning's progress, comes to the door of RICHARD'S apartment and rings the bell to warn him of her presence.

CLARISSA
Richard, Richard, it's me. I'm early. I know.

She puts her key in the lock and opens the door. The blinds have been pulled up and the curtains parted for the first time. In full light at last, it looks like the apartment of a madman—piles of cardboard boxes, a filthy bathtub, books flung everywhere. CLARISSA moves forward in astonishment.

CLARISSA
Richard! What the hell's going on?

RICHARD
What are you doing here? You're early.

RICHARD is pushing furniture to the side. He looks like an exalted scarecrow, his hair plastered to his skull. He's high as a kite, and still dressed in his bathrobe and pajamas. Immediately behind him, he has opened the window wide. CLARISSA looks in horror.

CLARISSA
Richard, what are you doing? What's going on?

RICHARD looks at her from across the room, his eyes gleaming.

RICHARD

Clarissa, I had this wonderful idea. I needed some light. I needed to let in some light.

RICHARD moves towards the window.

CLARISSA

Richard, what are you doing?

RICHARD

I had this fantastic notion. I took the Xanax *and* the Ritalin together. It had never occurred to me.

CLARISSA

Richard!

RICHARD screams at her.

RICHARD

Don't come near me!

CLARISSA stops. RICHARD scrambles painfully to the windowsill and lifts one leg over the sill, so that he is perched, bony, weightless, with the other foot still on the apartment floor. CLARISSA stands, trying to be calm.

RICHARD

It seemed to me I needed to let in some light. What do you think? I cleared away all the windows.

CLARISSA

All right, do me one favor, Richard, do me one simple favor . . .

RICHARD

I don't think I can make it to the party, Clarissa. I'm sorry.

CLARISSA

You don't have to go to the party. You don't have to go to the ceremony.

RICHARD'S face darkens. CLARISSA shouts in desperation.

CLARISSA

You don't have to do anything, Richard! You can do what you like!

RICHARD

But I have to face the hours, don't I? The hours after the party. And the hours after that.

CLARISSA

You have good days still, Richard. You know you do.

RICHARD

Not really. It's kind of you to say so, but it isn't true.

CLARISSA is stopped dead, full of fear at her next question.

CLARISSA

Are they here, Richard?

RICHARD

Who?

CLARISSA

The voices?

RICHARD

Oh, the voices are always here.

CLARISSA

But is it the voices you're hearing now?

                    RICHARD

No, Mrs. Dalloway. It's you.

CLARISSA looks at him, terrified now.

                    RICHARD

I've stayed alive for you.

RICHARD looks at her pleadingly.

                    RICHARD

But now you have to let me go.

CLARISSA looks at him, shocked by what he has said. But again as she
moves towards him, he cuts her off.

                    CLARISSA

Richard . . .

                    RICHARD

Tell me a story, all right?

                    CLARISSA

What about?

                    RICHARD

Tell me a story from your day.

CLARISSA stops, fearing this is their last moment together.

                    CLARISSA

I got up . . .

                    RICHARD

Yes?

And . . . I went out to get flowers—just like Mrs. Dalloway—in the book, do you know?

RICHARD

Yes.

CLARISSA

—it was a beautiful morning.

RICHARD

Was it?

CLARISSA

Yes. It was beautiful. It was so fresh.

CLARISSA shakes her head.

RICHARD

Fresh, was it?

CLARISSA

Yes.

RICHARD

Like a morning on the beach?

CLARISSA

Yes.

RICHARD

Like that?

CLARISSA

Yes.

RICHARD

Fresh like when you and I were young?

There is a silence. CLARISSA doesn't answer.

RICHARD

Like the morning you walked out of that old house and you
were eighteen, and maybe I was nineteen.

CLARISSA

Yes.

RICHARD

I was nineteen years old and I'd never seen anything so beautiful. You, coming out of a glass door in the early morning, still
sleepy. Isn't it strange?

CLARISSA

Yes. Yes it's strange.

RICHARD

The most ordinary morning in anybody's life.

RICHARD shakes his head slightly.

RICHARD

Clarissa, I'm afraid I can't make the party.

CLARISSA

The party doesn't matter. Give me your hand.

CLARISSA reaches out to him.

RICHARD

You've been so good to me, Mrs. Dalloway.

CLARISSA

Richard . . .

RICHARD

I love you.

CLARISSA stops, taken aback as he says it.

RICHARD

I don't think two people could have been happier than we've
been.

There is a moment's silence. Then RICHARD inches forward, slides gen-
tly off the sill, and falls. CLARISSA screams.

CLARISSA

No!

85. EXT. TRIANGLE BUILDING.
    EVE.

Silence. No sound. Seen from below, RICHARD'S body floating slowly
down from the fifth floor in the air.

86. INT. RICHARD'S APARTMENT.
    EVE.

CLARISSA looks at the empty window. Then she steps back away from
the window, just staring, making no noise. She takes one step back and
then another.

87. EXT. HUDSON STREET.
    EVE.

RICHARD'S body lands against the concrete, smashing a beer bottle as it does. The corpse bounces, then settles, face down, his robe up over his face. Silence again.

88. INT. BROWNS' HOUSE.
    NIGHT.

1951. The cake, now bright with lit candles on the dining-room table. A great effort has been made for DAN'S birthday and the front room is bright with light and decoration. DAN blows out his candles in one long go. RICHIE and LAURA watch from their seats at the table.

                    RICHIE & LAURA
Happy Birthday! Happy Birthday, Dan!

They all laugh.

                        DAN
This is perfect. This is just perfect.

                        LAURA
Do you think so? Do you really think so?

                        DAN
Why sure. You must have been working all day.

                        LAURA
Well we were. Weren't we, bug? That's what we were doing.
Working all day.

                        DAN
This is just fantastic. It's what I've always wanted.

LAURA is doing well as the good wife, sharing her husband's delight in the cake. RICHIE is watching, with a serious expression.

LAURA

Oh Dan . . .

DAN

One day I'll tell you, Richie, I'll tell you how it all happened . . .

LAURA

Don't.

LAURA seems embarrassed. DAN looks up at her, quiet but serious.

DAN

I want to. I want to tell him the story.

LAURA is silent, giving permission, but ill at ease. DAN looks at RICHIE, full of pleasure at picking his way exactly through his story.

DAN

What happened: when I was at war—at war I found myself thinking—and I remembered that there was this girl that I'd seen—I'd never met her—at High School—this strange, fragile-looking girl called Laura McGrath. Yeah. And she was shy. And she was interesting. And—your mother won't mind me saying this, Richie—she was the kind of girl you see sitting mostly on her own.

RICHIE is listening intently. The three of them are intent round the table.

DAN

Yes. Richie, I'll tell you: sometimes when I was in the South Pacific, the fact is, I used to think of this girl . . .

LAURA

Dan . . .

DAN

I thought of bringing her to a house—a life—well, pretty like this. And it was the thought of the happiness . . . the thought of this woman . . . the thought of this life . . . that is what sustained me.

There is silence. DAN is looking at LAURA

DAN

I had an idea of our happiness.

RICHIE watches, aware of the awful sadness between them.

LAURA

Did you make a wish?

DAN has taken one of the yellow roses from the cake, and, unaware, has been rolling it between his fingers, back and forth, back and forth. He is alone with his thoughts for a few moments, then he turns and looks blankly at LAURA. Then he nods.

DAN

Yes, I did.

89. INT. MORGUE.
NIGHT.

CLARISSA is seen through the glass panel in a door waiting at the morgue. She is standing in distress, shaken by the events of the afternoon. Then SALLY arrives at the door, led into the morgue by an ORDERLY. She stops a moment to look through the door. Now, full of feeling, she opens the door to join CLARISSA. CLARISSA looks across.

90. INT. HOGARTH HOUSE.
NIGHT.

In the drawing room, there are two pools of light from standard lamps. On opposite sides of the room LEONARD and VIRGINIA are sitting, a kind of truce between them after the events of the afternoon. They are both reading. VIRGINIA'S book is in her hand. She still has the London rail ticket, which she is using as a bookmark. She fingers the ticket, turning it over. After a few moments LEONARD looks up, as if something has occurred to him from a previous conversation.

LEONARD

Why does someone have to die?

VIRGINIA looks up and frowns.

VIRGINIA

Leonard?

LEONARD

In your book?

VIRGINIA

Oh.

LEONARD

You said someone has to die. Why?

LEONARD catches just a trace of VIRGINIA'S reaction.

LEONARD

Is that a stupid question?

VIRGINIA

No.

LEONARD

I imagine my question is stupid.

                              VIRGINIA

Not at all.

                              LEONARD

Well?

VIRGINIA gives it thought before answering.

                              VIRGINIA

Someone has to die in order that the rest of us should value life
more.

LEONARD looks at her, the two of them serious now.

                              VIRGINIA

It's contrast.

                              LEONARD

And who will die?

                              VIRGINIA

It's a secret.

                              LEONARD

Tell me.

VIRGINIA pauses, then gives him the gift of an answer.

                              VIRGINIA

The poet will die. The visionary.

91. INT. BROWNS' HOUSE. RICHIE'S BEDROOM.
     NIGHT.

1951. RICHIE, the poet, the visionary, lying in the bed in a little room painted with stars. It is decorated with pictures of rockets and imaginary astronauts. His face is alert on the pillow.

92. EXT. BROWNS' HOUSE.
NIGHT.

The Browns' house seen from the road. It's dark. Just one pool of light is thrown onto their drive by a side-window. The street at peace.

93. INT. BROWNS' HOUSE. RICHIE'S BEDROOM.
NIGHT.

RICHIE is lying awake listening to the sound of his father in the next room calling to LAURA.

94. INT. BROWNS' HOUSE. BATHROOM.
NIGHT.

LAURA is sitting, her head in her hands, on the closed toilet seat. She is in white pajamas, bent down in an attitude of abject despair, unable to move. After a few moments, DAN calls through from the bedroom.

DAN (*bedroom*)

What are you doing?

LAURA looks up. She has taken her make-up off and it is plain she has been crying.

LAURA

I'm brushing my teeth.

DAN (*bedroom*)

Are you coming to bed?

LAURA

Yes. In a minute.

DAN (*bedroom*)

Come to bed, Laura Brown.

But LAURA doesn't move, just turns away, trapped.

DAN (*bedroom*)

I ran into Ray, he says Kitty's had to go to the hospital.

LAURA

That's right.

DAN (*bedroom*)

Nothing serious, he said. Just a checkup.

LAURA

I'm terrified.

DAN (*bedroom*)

Why?

LAURA speaks quietly, not loud enough for DAN to hear.

LAURA

Oh, the idea she could vanish.

DAN has not heard anything.

DAN (*bedroom*)

Perhaps you could go see her in the morning, honey.

LAURA

I was going to. I was going to stop by.

There is another short silence. LAURA is unable to move.

DAN (*bedroom*)

I've had a wonderful day and I have you to thank.

LAURA looks away, in despair now.

DAN (*bedroom*)

Come to bed, honey.

LAURA

I'm coming.

But still LAURA stands, not moving. After a while, DAN speaks again.

DAN (*bedroom*)

So. Are you coming?

LAURA

Yes.

In the distance, you can hear a dog barking. LAURA gets up and reaches for the pull-light over the mirror. The bathroom goes dark. She takes the steps which bring her to the door which leads to the bedroom. LAURA stands in the door, the only light falling on her face.

95. INT. HOGARTH HOUSE. STUDY.
    DAY.

1923. VIRGINIA is now sitting in her favorite chair with a writing board across her lap, notebook in hand. The light pools around her. She is not writing, just thinking. LEONARD appears in the doorway opposite. He says nothing.

VIRGINIA

What? What?

LEONARD smiles.

                              LEONARD

I was hoping you were going to bed.

                              VIRGINIA

I am. I am going to bed.

They look at each other, their eyes full of love and humor.

                              LEONARD

What then?

                              VIRGINIA

All else is clear. The outline of the story is planned. Now one
thing only.

VIRGINIA shakes her head very slightly, still in the chair.

                              VIRGINIA

Mrs. Dalloway's destiny must be resolved.

96. INT. CLARISSA'S APARTMENT.
    NIGHT.

2001. CLARISSA is in the kitchen with SALLY and JULIA. Every surface
is taken up with food for the party which never happened. CLARISSA has
the crab dish in her hand and is emptying it sadly into the bin. She is still
in the coat she was wearing all afternoon. As she dumps the wasted food,
she hears a ring at the door.

CLARISSA goes to the apartment door and opens it. LAURA BROWN is
standing directly opposite. She is now in her early 80s, slightly stooped
with steel-gray hair and parchment skin. She is wearing a dark, floral
dress and coat. CLARISSA is taken aback for a moment.

                              CLARISSA

You're Laura Brown.

LAURA

Yes. I'm Richard's mother.

CLARISSA

Of course.

CLARISSA reaches out her hand.

CLARISSA

I'm Clarissa Vaughan. Come in.

LAURA has a small bag which CLARISSA now lifts for her as she leads her into the apartment. At the end of the corridor SALLY is standing with JULIA behind her, but CLARISSA signals tactfully for them to hold off a moment, as she leads LAURA into the sitting room. Throughout the apartment, dinner tables have been set with white table cloths, and glasses. CLARISSA is alone with LAURA in the sitting room.

CLARISSA

My friend Sally's in the kitchen. And my daughter.

LAURA just looks at her a moment, not answering.

CLARISSA

We were having a party. We were going to have a party.

LAURA

I was lucky. I got the last plane from Toronto.

In the kitchen, unheard, unseen, JULIA watches, then speaks quietly to SALLY.

JULIA

So that's the monster.

LAURA has approached a table loaded with RICHARD'S books.

CLARISSA

I hope I did the right thing. I found your number in his phone book.

LAURA

Yes. He had it. But we didn't speak often.

LAURA is looking at RICHARD'S picture. CLARISSA stands a moment, waiting.

LAURA

It's a terrible thing, Miss Vaughan, to outlive your whole family.

CLARISSA

Richard's father died . . .

LAURA

Yes. He died of cancer. Quite young. And Richard's sister is dead.

LAURA looks at her a moment.

LAURA

Obviously you feel unworthy. It gives you feelings of unworthiness. You survive and they don't.

CLARISSA waits a second before speaking.

CLARISSA

Did you read the poems?

LAURA

Yes. I read them. I also read the novel. You see, people say that the novel is difficult . . .

CLARISSA

I know . . .

LAURA

They say that.

CLARISSA

I know . . .

LAURA

He had me die in the novel. I know why he did that. It hurt, of course. I can't pretend it didn't hurt, but I know why he did it.

CLARISSA

You left Richard when he was a child?

LAURA

I left both my children. I abandoned them. They say it's the worst thing a mother can do.

Neither of them move. The room is silent now.

LAURA

You have a daughter?

CLARISSA

Yes. But I never met Julia's father.

LAURA

You so wanted a child?

CLARISSA

That's right.

LAURA

You're a very lucky woman.

CLARISSA looks down.

There are times when you don't belong and you think you're going to kill yourself. Once I went to a hotel. That night . . . later that night, I made a plan. Plan was, I would leave my family when my second child was born. And that's what I did. Got up one morning, made breakfast, went to the bus stop, got on a bus. I'd left a note.

There's a moment's silence.

I got a job in a library in Canada. It would be wonderful to say you regretted it. It would be easy. But what does it mean? What does it mean to regret when you have no choice? It's what you can bear. There it is. No one is going to forgive me.

LAURA looks at CLARISSA, steady, unapologetic.

It was death. I chose life.

97. INT. CLARISSA'S APARTMENT.
NIGHT.

CLARISSA comes out of the sitting room down the hall of the apartment and quietly goes into their bedroom, still wearing her dark coat. SALLY is in the kitchen with JULIA and now looks up at the sight of CLARISSA. She gets up and follows CLARISSA into the bedroom.

98. INT. CLARISSA'S APARTMENT. BEDROOM.
NIGHT.

SALLY comes into the room to find CLARISSA sitting on the side of the bed in her coat. The two women look at each other.

SALLY

You need to take your coat off.

SALLY comes round and gestures to CLARISSA to stand up. SALLY puts her hands on CLARISSA'S shoulders to help her take off the coat. As she does, CLARISSA turns and looks at SALLY, the two of them overcome. The two women look warmly at each other, then they kiss.

99. INT. APARTMENT. JULIA'S BEDROOM. NIGHT.

LAURA is unpacking her suitcase on the bed in Julia's room. It has only a few things which she has hurriedly put in for the trip. She looks frail and alone. There is a knock on the door and JULIA comes in with a cup and saucer.

JULIA

I thought you might like a cup of tea.

LAURA

That's very kind, dear. I feel I'm stealing your room.

JULIA has put the tea down beside the bed.

JULIA

We put the food away, so . . . if you're hungry in the night, just help yourself.

LAURA

Well, I will. You have somewhere?

JULIA

Yes. The sofa.

LAURA

I'm sorry.

Instinctively JULIA moves towards her and puts her arms round her. The 18 year-old and the 80 year-old embrace. LAURA stands a moment, astonished at her warmth. Then JULIA moves away.

> LAURA

Good night, sweetheart.

> JULIA

Good night.

100. INT. HOGARTH HOUSE. BEDROOM. NIGHT.

1923. VIRGINIA lies in bed, making no effort to sleep, but lying by moonlight in her bed, her eyes open, white like a ghost.

101. INT. CLARISSA'S APARTMENT. KITCHEN. NIGHT.

2001. The corridor of the apartment. Everyone else has gone to bed. CLARISSA, in her white pajamas, is in the kitchen turning off the lights one by one. As she turns off the last one in the kitchen, she comes into the corridor, and begins the same process. She looks round briefly at her own home: comfortable, solid, complete. At last she seems at peace. As she turns out the lights in the corridor, the voice of VIRGINIA WOOLF is heard.

> VIRGINIA (v.o.)

Dear Leonard, to look life in the face, always to look life in the face, and to know what it is, to love it for what it is. At last to know it. To love it for what it is. And then to put it away.

CLARISSA turns out the last light and the corridor is darkened. She turns and goes into her room.

102. EXT. RIVER OUSE.
    DAY.

1941. VIRGINIA WOOLF walks calmly once more into the river.

VIRGINIA (*v.o.*)
Leonard, always the years between us, always the years, always
the love. Always the hours.

VIRGINIA stands a moment, up to her neck in the water, about to
plunge herself under. The sun plays on the water.

FADE.